W9-AGK-558

MYSTERIOUS BRITAIN

Homer Sykes

MYSTERIOUS BRITAIN

Fact and Folklore

Weidenfeld and Nicolson

London

For Judy, Theo, Jacob and Tallulah

Text and photographs copyright © Homer Sykes 1993

First published in 1993 by George Weidenfeld and Nicolson Ltd,
The Orion Publishing Group, Orion House, 5 Upper St Martin's Lane,
London, WC2H 9EA

All rights reserved. No part of this publication may be reproduced, stored in
a retrieval system, or transmitted, in any form or by any means, electronic,
mechanical, photocopying, or otherwise, without the prior permission of the
copyright owner.

British Library Cataloguing in Publication Data
A catalogue record for this book is available from the British Library

Title Page: The Graveyard, Nr South Zeal, Devon

Printed and bound in Italy

Contents

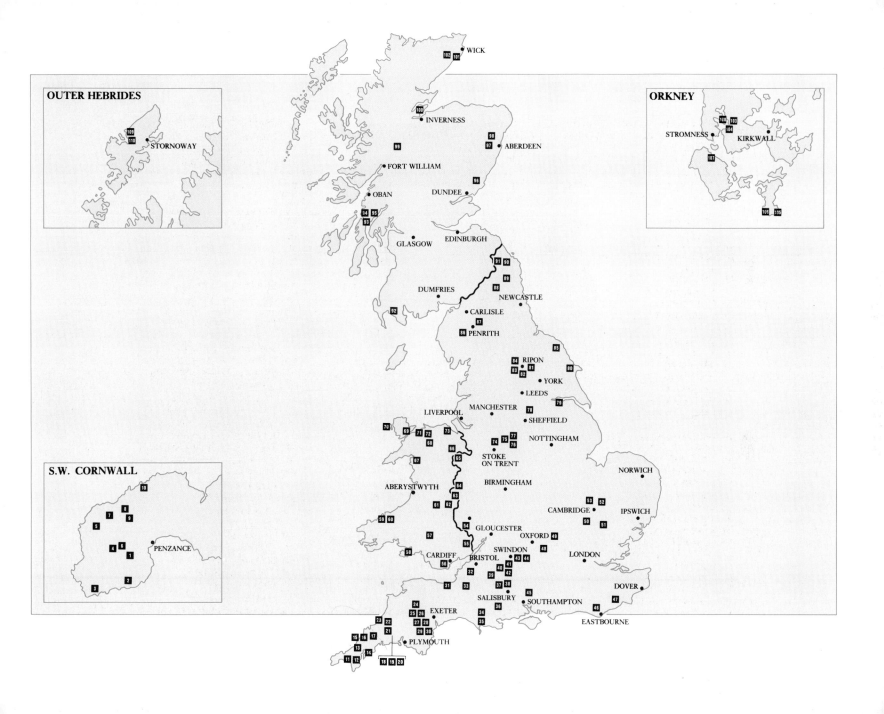

INTRODUCTION

Britain has more prehistoric monuments than any other European country but, although many thousands of people visit Stonehenge each year, how many of these intrigued visitors know of any other sites? A few may have visited Avebury and an even smaller number may have climbed Silbury Hill, both only a short distance from Stonehenge. A tiny percentage might have heard of the Callanish Standing Stones, but do they know where they are?

Many of the prehistoric monuments and more recent sites photographed have become associated with folklore, legend and mystery. These legends and folktales stem from the period of the introduction of Christianity into Britain. In many cases folktales were introduced to explain why the new Christian faith had embraced prehistoric pagan monuments. Other stories were developed to illustrate the power of the new religion over the old. Nevertheless pagan ideas did not die easily and throughout Britain certain aspects of pagan culture can still be found in places of Christian worship today.

There is a remarkable similarity in legends and stories associated with prehistoric monuments, and these can be heard throughout Britain. For example, there are two main stories associated with standing stones: firstly, that a devil or giant became angry with the new Christians and took it upon himself to destroy them and their church by hurling a huge rock at them, which never hit its mark. The Devil's Arrows at Boroughbridge, North Yorkshire, are supposedly three bolts that were fired by the Devil at the citizens of an early Christian settlement, Aldborough. At Trelleck, in Gwent, Harold's Stones – three large, aligned standing stones – were thrown down by the giant Jack O'Kent while he was playing Pitch and Toss with the Devil.

The second theme, and the one that is most common in the south-west of England, is that standing stones and stone circles are comprised of miscreants who failed to attend

STONEHENGE,
Nr Amesbury, Wiltshire
The Heel Stone is said to have got its name after the Devil saw a monk spying on him. He hurled the rock, which caught the monk on the heel, pinning him to the ground. On the morning of the summer solstice the sun rises over the Heel Stone.

church on the Sabbath. The Merry Maidens and their Pipers near Lamorna in Cornwall are typical of this folktale. Two large, single, phallic standing stones are said to be evil pagan spirits who beguiled nineteen maidens from a nearby village into going dancing rather than going to church. Their punishment for non-attendance was to be turned to stone – a perpetual reminder to others of the power of the Church. One of the many folktales associated with the Callanish Standing Stones on the Isle of Lewis, probably second only in importance to Stonehenge, has it that they represent thirteen local giants who refused to join the new church. This band of reprobates were turned to stone as an example to the other islanders.

Sanctifying ancient and venerated sites was common and no doubt gave the first converts from paganism a sense of continuity. There are several examples of churches being built within henges and stone circles, and some include single standing stones within their boundaries. In Scotland the eighteenth-century Church of Christ at Midmar was built only a short way away from the chapel founded in the sixth century by Saint Nidan, and the chapel was in turn erected next to a Bronze Age recumbent stone circle. In fact one of the larger stones from the circle was taken down and probably used in the construction of the church's foundations. At Knowlton in Dorset a twelfth-century church was built within a Neolithic henge and, at Rudston in Humberside, All Saints Church was built within yards of Britain's tallest monolith. The name Rudston derives from the old English words *rood* meaning cross and *stan* meaning stone. It is quite probable that early Christian missionaries attached a wooden cross to the top of the monolith to 'convert' it.

These prehistoric monuments were built by Neolithic and Bronze Age man for ritual purposes. It is believed that they worshipped the sun which gave warmth and light, and water, a life-giving force. Water was also worshipped for its magical curative powers. Many prehistoric monuments are aligned to the sun and the moon; for example in the Orkneys and Outer Hebrides, both the Ring of Brodgar and the Callanish Standing Stones are. In England of course Stonehenge, probably the most famous of the prehistoric monuments, has been regarded by many as an astronomical computer

NORMANTON DOWN BARROW CEMETERY,
Nr Amesbury, Wiltshire

There are over three hundred barrows built by Bronze Age man between 1700 and 1400 BC clustered around Stonehenge like stars around a planet, each holding many secrets. These round barrows are in contrast to the communal burial places of Neolithic man, the long barrows. Burial took place at first by inhumation, the body being laid in a crouching position, and then by cremation, often in specially-built 'houses of the dead', or in the person's own home, along with urns containing food offerings. These barrows have been known to contain tin, glazed earthenware, beads from the Near East, amber from the British coast, shale from Dorset, daggers in wooden and leather sheaths, and even, sewn onto one corpse, a lozenge-shaped plate of sheet gold. Surely this is the last resting place of a fabulous, powerful and wealthy Wessex tribe.

aligned to the movements of the sun, moon and stars, though these alignments are now known to be imprecise.

Other prehistoric monuments are associated with death and afterlife. The Neolithic long barrow, for example, was often used for up to a thousand years for the burial of a tribe's dead, and in this respect it can be likened to our churches and cathedrals.

Some of the most impressive places in this book have become associated with Druids – the Celtic High Priests of pre-Christian Britain, Ireland and Gaul. They venerated sacred oak groves and held secret ritual gatherings where human sacrifices were offered to appease the spirit gods. Through a state of trance the Druids were able to enter the animistic world, in which inanimate objects such as trees or monoliths were considered to have human souls. Stonehenge, Avebury and other megalithic sites became associated with the Druids who undoubtedly used these temples for their rituals, and were aware of their astrological significance.

These pagan Celts were headhunters, subscribing to the 'cult of the head', which was considered a potent symbol of divine persona. The custom of gilding an enemy's skull and using it as a drinking vessel was common. Until recently, this Celtic practice was evident at St Teilo's Well, where water was renowned for its special properties, but only if drunk from the remains of St Teilo's skull. There are many legends of springs issuing forth from the spot where a decapitated head had fallen. In Scotland, at Invergarry, the Head Well is marked with the decapitated heads of seven men. The practice of depicting holy water with a headless body can still be found on some ancient fonts, in, for example, the Church of St Gwrthwl at Llanwrthwl, Powys, and also on the font at St Germoe Church in Cornwall. In some places, water is still venerated. The spring water of the Cloutie Well at Munlochy is said to be a cure-all (particularly potent on the first of May), provided a cloth rag is left as a gift in place of the water. Legend has it that anyone who destroys or removes the rags, or clouties, will fall ill with the donor's ailment.

Celtic holy men who sailed from Ireland to England, and journeyed through Wales and Scotland, in the first centuries AD set up oratories and baptistries. These 'saints' –

UFFINGTON WHITE HORSE,
Nr Wantage, Oxfordshire
The Uffington White Horse is the earliest and largest of the Wessex White Horses. It is 360 feet long and is cut into the chalk on the north-facing crest of an escarpment below the Iron Age hill fort known as Uffington Castle, now dated to approximately 50 BC. The horse was a powerful symbol to the Celts and may well have been the tribal symbol of the Atrebates, carved on the hillside to protect them. There are many legends associated with this White Horse, first mentioned in 1084. Some see it not as a horse but as the dragon that St George killed. Where its blood spilled on nearby flat-topped Dragon Hill, it is said that no grass has ever grown.

the title comes from the Latin *sanctus* meaning holy and it is not a status conferred by the Catholic Church – taught and baptized heathens into the Christian faith. They often conducted funerals and their followers were buried near the first small churches.

Many early churches have pagan effigies carved into their fabric. These stone and wood carvings often mean little to us nowadays, and are forgotten high in the roof or in some dark recess at the back of the church. But the meaning was clear to craftsmen who knew their work would live on. Just why the Green Man, a Celtic fertility symbol, or the explicit and grotesque effigy known as a Sheela-na-gig, a Celtic goddess of creation and destruction, or the sexual imagery of tongue-poking gargoyles were permissible remains a mystery. Many of these images have been destroyed, while others have been copied, adapted and corrupted so that their original meaning has been lost. Those stone carvings that have been exposed to the elements have often weathered so much that their explicitness is no longer visible. Some have been boarded up, but others are now on view again; for example the Sheela-na-gig figure on the rood screen at St Mary and All Saints Church in Willingham, Cambridgeshire (described in the church leaflet as an 'imp'!). The unique and beautifully carved Dragon and Green Man bench-ends at the Church of the Holy Ghost in Crowcombe, Somerset, are also well worth visiting.

During the fifteenth century it became common for the iconography of death to be shown in the most macabre fashion. Cadaverous tombs, of which there are 154 left in Britain, are a style within the general genre of memento mori – a reminder of the inevitability of death, and, underlying the practice, the belief that in the eye of God, regardless of wealth and position, we are all the same.

These three-, two- and single-tier tombs were popular for about a hundred years. The upper tier would show the deceased in all their finery, indicating their position in society. A knight, for example, would be shown in his finest armour, with his sword, coat of arms and perhaps a dog at his feet. Below this would be the effigy of a corpse, wrapped only in a shroud, often in an advanced state of decay, and sometimes skeletal.

During the eighteenth and nineteenth centuries it became fashionable in some circles to be associated with a Druidic revival. This Neodruidism was spearheaded by John

Aubrey and William Stukeley, the latter becoming preoccupied with the cult and eventually taking holy orders in the belief that it was his divine mission to reconcile Druidism and Christianity. Societies flourished, many claiming to be the rightful inheritors of the traditional knowledge of the early Druids. The Neolithic burial chamber in Anglesey, Bryn Celli Ddu – 'hill of the dark grove' – became the scene of Druidic revival, so too the weirdly-shaped Brimham Rocks, and Midmar Stone Circle, with a recumbent stone looking not unlike a sacrificial altar, which became known as The Druids.

This revival coincided with a new enthusiasm for antiquarianism, which developed alongside the Romantic movement in literature and art. This period was also the Age of the Folly. Following the example set by Sir John Vanbrugh and Nicholas Hawksmoor at Castle Howard numerous rich landowners, influenced by contemporary art and continental travel, embraced the view that the great country parks could be enhanced with the addition of a Greek parthenon, Roman ruin, Egyptian pyramid or Druid temple. These structures started to appear, acting as eyecatchers to punctuate the landscape, built to impress, amuse and on occasion to create work for estate labourers. William Danby, having returned from a European tour 'where he saw a real one', started to build a Druids temple a few miles north of his country mansion, Swinton Hall near Masham in North Yorkshire. In Shropshire, Major West who owned large estates, was having his own Druid temple built, though this was not as spectacular as the Danby example, and has now fallen into ruin. At about the same time, Mad Jack Fuller was spending his last years creating a series of follies on his estate at Brightling in East Sussex. A church tower known as the Sugar Loaf was erected so he might win a wager; a mausoleum was constructed, modelled on the Tomb of Cestius in Rome, where according to local legend, Mad Jack was buried in full evening dress, seated at a laid table with his hand outstretched to a bottle of port. At about the same time, in Hampshire, Squire Paulet St John, a relation of Mad Jack's, was building a pyramid as a memorial for his horse, Chalk Pit. Perhaps a modern legend to echo that of King Sil and his golden horse at Silbury Hill.

ENGLAND

Standing at the Heel Stone and looking with awe at Britain's best-known prehistoric monument – Stonehenge – on a bitingly cold but golden winter evening, it is easy to imagine this temple as it was, at the centre of a great farming community, rich with bronze and trade.

According to Professor Richard Atkinson who carried out the first detailed excavations in the 1950s, Stonehenge was built in three phases over 700 years. 2200 BC saw the first simple henge monument being built by Neolithic man. A huge circular enclosure was constructed, 900 feet across with an internal quarry ditch and bank. An enormous thirty-two-ton sarsen stone was erected at the entrance to the north-east. Now called the Heel Stone, it is the only naturally weathered stone in the complex. Fifty-six pits were dug within the henge, known as the Aubrey Holes after the seventeenth-century archaeologist who first discovered them. These were filled with blood and human remains. Burial pits or sacrificial pits with offerings to appease the gods? We will never know.

Some five hundred years later, the community having grown and prospered, Bronze Age Beaker people started what is now considered the second phase. Eighty Blue Stones, each weighing about four tons, were transported from the Prescelly Mountains in Dyfed, Wales, and erected in a circle within the Neolithic henge. To bring these stones nearly 200 miles was a colossal task, and must have taken an inordinate amount of planning, manpower, skill and above else determination. One has to ask, why did they do it? No conclusive answer has ever been given. There are many sites much closer where stone could have been quarried. Could the Prescelly Mountains have been holy? Did Bronze Age man believe that the Blue Stones, when freshly cut, had some special religious significance, some properties, perhaps magical, they understood but we do not?

AVEBURY STONE,
Avebury, Wiltshire
The West Kennet Avenue leads from Avebury henge and stone circle to the sanctuary one and a half miles away. Probably built as a processional route, this avenue now consists of thirty pairs of stones, some of which are diamond shaped.

Just how they got them to Stonehenge is an extraordinary feat of prehistoric engineering. It has been suggested that they were dragged to the sea, and then taken along the Welsh coast slung between two boats, then up the River Severn, and overland on a series of log rollers, heaved and pushed by teams of men. It would have taken many years.

The third and final phase was probably at the command of the great Wessex chiefs who ruled this area. Numerous rich barrows surround Stonehenge, testament to their wealth. This phase saw the redesigning of the stone circle, in which the Blue Stones were taken down, and eighty sarsen stones, each weighing up to fifty tons, brought overland from a site twenty miles away, near Avebury. It has been estimated that this task would have taken a thousand men working every day ten years to accomplish. When on site these sarsen stones were mauled into shape, and tongue and groove joints cut. Each block could have taken as many as fifty men five years to shape and complete. Thirty of these were then tipped and fixed into holes already cut. The horizontal lintels were moved upwards inch by inch on a series of wooden ramps and finally pushed and secured into place. These trilithons are what we see today. Stonehenge was complete.

But what is Stonehenge? In many people's minds it is associated with the Druids. They undoubtedly used Stonehenge for their rituals, but we know that they did not build it. They came to Salisbury Plain 2000 years after its inception. Hundreds of theories have been put forward, proposing everything from waystations for UFOs to giant computers for predicting eclipses. One theory has recently been suggested by Dr Terence Meaden in his book *The Stonehenge Solution*. He puts forward the theory that the temple was dedicated to the Sky God and the Great Mother Goddess, worshipped by the ancients. He argues that the temple was for the annual consummation of their marriage, which would have symbolized a prosperous new year. He bases this theory around the Heel Stone which, shortly after a midsummer sunrise, casts a long and phallic shadow right into the centre, the 'womb', of the temple. Just another theory? If correct we will never know; the Stonehenge enigma will probably remain for ever.

Some of the most magical and mysterious prehistoric monuments, though much smaller than Stonehenge, can be found near the remote, beautiful and diminutive

NINE MAIDENS STONE CIRCLE,
Nr Tregeseal, Cornwall

This is all that remains of what was once a triple circle formation, possibly similar to the Hurlers on Bodmin Moor. One of the circles was only recently discovered after careful study of aerial photographs, while the other was damaged in the nineteenth century, then completely destroyed in the 1960s when extensive field clearance took place. Nevertheless the Tregeseal Nine Maidens Circle is quite beautiful and evocative. Presumably these Maidens danced, like their sisters, the Merry Maidens in Lamorna, on the Sabbath and were also turned into stone for their sin.

granite village of Zennor in Cornwall, perched on the cliffs overlooking the Atlantic: next stop America. In this rugged country where the wind bites through you in winter, and in summer the sun seems rarely to set, it is not difficult to imagine prehistoric man carving out and creating a culture that we still do not, and probably never will, fully understand. Near here can be found fragments of an exciting and wonderful past – Lanyon, Mulfra and Chun Quoit; the Merry Maidens and their Pipers, the Blind Fiddler and the Two Sisters; Men Scryfa, the Iron Age Carn Euny Fogou, the Men-an-Tol and many other prehistoric monuments.

A few miles away, across Penwith Moor, is the mysterious Men-an-Tol. This and other 'holed' stones have been credited with possessing magical, curative powers. Ceremonies have to be performed for their magic to work. Many different types of illness can be cured, and fertility and potency stimulated. The Men-an-Tol was once known as the Crick Stone, though the alignment as we see it today was probably effected in the nineteenth century. The 'female' stone was said to be able to cure back pain, but only if the afflicted person crawled through the aperture nine times. Young children were baptized by being passed through the stone naked.

At Tolvan Cross there is an enigmatic, seven-and-a-half-foot, triangular granite stone known, like the Men-an-Tol, for its curative powers. When dowsed, forces of energy definitely passed through it. How the hole was made remains a mystery. Today, even with modern power tools, drilling through twelve inches of granite would be no easy task, let alone creating a perfectly circular aperture, with a smooth bevelled edge.

Both the Men-an-Tol and the Tolvan Stone are uncannily similar, and how Bronze Age man managed this is baffling to modern minds. As to the stones' purpose, it has been suggested that they were originally used to block some now-lost, prehistoric burial tomb, the hole allowing a way in for funerary purposes, and a passage out for the spirit of the dead.

The Merry Maidens and their Pipers, the Blind Fiddler and the Two Sisters, the Hurlers and the Nine Stones on Dartmoor are just a few of the prehistoric monuments where, according to legend, people have been turned to stone – their sin, non-attendance at church on a Sunday. The Sabbath they celebrated instead, however, was probably a witches' sabbath. In the Middle Ages a coven of witches – both men and women – met and were led in their rituals by a 'high priest' disguised as some loathsome beast. All would announce the evil they had performed since they last met. Feasting on a murdered child's flesh, dancing and drinking potent brews, an orgy of depravity ensued. It is not surprising that the Church tried to scare the local people into ending these pagan ways.

Knowlton Henge in Dorset is a desolate and beautiful place. The Neolithic henge, one of an original set of three, but preserved and particularly special because of the twelfth-century church built within its banks, is a pagan temple, Christianized and now abandoned. I watched white witches gather here and, in silence and single file, walk in an anticlockwise procession right around the outer bank, before dowsing the henge to release 'trapped energies'.

At Rudston there is Britain's tallest prehistoric monument – over twenty feet high and now wearing a lead cap for protection. The giant's smaller partner can be found tucked away in the corner of Rudston churchyard, surrounded by rotting grass cuttings, dead flowers and a broken tombstone. Once this must have been the centre of a flourishing Bronze Age community; little now remains, save the giant monolith and its partner, testament to the power of the Church over paganism.

TRETHEVY QUOIT, *Nr St Cleer, Cornwall*

Trethevy Quoit, Cornwall's largest and, some say, most impressive Neolithic monument, stands alone on its small mound in a field behind the village of St Cleer with its Holy Well. Towering fifteen feet high, this magnificent double-chambered tomb has variously been known as King Arthur's Quoit and the Giant's House. The huge capstone, twelve and a half feet long, is now supported by six uprights, the seventh having fallen into the antichamber, thus causing the dangerous degree at which the structure now rests. Some say it looks as if it should have fallen in a thousand years ago. Uniquely, the vast blocking slab has had an angular hole cut into it; conceivably to allow bodies to be passed into the main chamber, or perhaps to allow food to be passed inside to sustain life after death.

LANYON QUOIT, *Nr Morvah, Cornwall*

Lanyon Quoit is within sight of the Morvah–Madron road, about half a mile from the Men-an-Tol, and for this reason is one of the best known quoits in Cornwall. This huge Neolithic chamber tomb, over six thousand years old, is wrongly supposed by some to be the most perfect in Cornwall. Unfortunately over the years treasure seekers have weakened the structure to such a degree that in a ferocious storm last century the capstone was dislodged and one of the upright stones broken. The whole tomb was reconstructed and the capstone, weighing over thirteen tons, replaced, using the same equipment that put the Logan Stone of Treen back in place. Prior to this, according to reports, a man on horseback could easily ride underneath without lowering his head. Legend has it that King Arthur took his last meal here before his final battle, and Merlin predicted that the King and his chieftains would meet here again before the end of the world.

CHUN QUOIT, *Nr Morvah, Cornwall*

Squatting on open moorland, not unlike a huge megalithic mushroom, Chun Quoit commands a dramatic view across windblown Penwith to Pendeen Watch and the Three Stones Oar in the Atlantic Ocean. This classic, nearly six-foot-tall, Neolithic chamber tomb is wonderfully preserved. The large convex capstone, measuring ten foot by nine, and two and a half feet thick, sits firmly on three large slabs, the fourth is now out of contact with the stone. Once partially covered with an oval or round mound of earth, this nine-ton granite monument is the last resting place of a great Neolithic leader. Only 300 yards away – but separated by a distance of 2000 years – is an Iron Age hill fort. It is remarkable that the quoit was not destroyed by the builders and settlers who lived there. Indeed, on the contrary, this exquisite quoit was held in great reverence by them.

WAYLAND'S SMITHY, *Uffington, Oxfordshire*

A few miles along the Ridgeway from the Uffington White Horse, a five-thousand-year-old burial chamber can be found, known as Wayland's Smithy. Saxon settlers came across the tomb and, not knowing what it was, presumed it to be the work of one of their gods, Wayland the Smith. With the advent of Christianity a legend grew up that the only way Wayland could make a living was to shoe moorland ponies, and that if you left your horse with a silver coin overnight it would be shod by morning.

The original tomb built on top of this chalk ridge held fifteen people in a large wooden chamber. This was oval in shape and completely covered over with chalk dug from side ditches, which were lined in stone. The burial

chamber could have served as a mark of ownership of the land by a local tribe, or else as a ceremonial place to link the living with the dead. 1700 years later a further tomb was built, completely covering the first. It was much bigger and at one end had stone-lined burial chambers. When it was opened in 1920 it was found to have been sacked, but amongst the jumble of bones left, the remains of eight people were found.

is constructed in steps, each step being filled in with packed chalk, and then smoothed off.

According to legend, this is the last resting place of King Sil and his fabled golden horse. Another legend claims that the mound holds a lifesize, solid gold statue of King Sil, and yet a third, that the Devil was carrying an apron of soil to drop on the citizens of Marlborough. He was spotted by the priests of nearby Avebury, who made him empty his apron before he got there. There have been three excavations of the mound; the first when a team of Cornish miners sunk a shaft from top to bottom in 1776, another in 1849 when a tunnel was dug from the edge into the centre, and a third in 1968–70 led by Professor Richard Atkinson. Nothing has ever been found.

SILBURY HILL, *Nr Marlborough, Wiltshire*

Very little is known about this, the largest man-made prehistoric mound in Europe, a few miles west of Marlborough on the A4. Conical in shape and covering five acres, it is 130 feet tall and 100 feet across its flat top. It has been estimated that it took eighteen million man-hours to construct. We know that building took place in two phases, dating from 2145 BC. Soon after work was started, a re-design was ordered, and the mound enlarged. It

CASTLERIGG STONE CIRCLE, *Nr Keswick, Cumbria*

The egg-shaped Castlerigg Stone Circle is 700 feet above sea level and dramatically set in an open field between the lakeland mountains of Skiddaw and Helvellyn. It is also known as the Keswick Carles and, according to Cumbrian folklore, consists of men turned to stone. A Neolithic and Bronze Age sacred meeting place, it is made up of 38 small stones, few of which are taller than four and a half feet. It has a wide entrance defined by two taller pillars. To the north and within the circle in the south-east sector is an enigmatic rectangle made up of ten stones.

ARBOR LOW, *Nr Youlgreave, Derbyshire*
Sometimes known as the 'Stonehenge of the Peaks', Arbor Low is an
exquisite and enigmatic henge and stone circle, lying on windswept
moorland just off the Buxton to Ashbourne road. Built by Bronze Age man
between 2500 and 1700 BC, this circle of over forty locally-cut limestone
blocks all now lie, like the face of an astronomical clock, on a raised plateau,
which is surrounded by a quarry ditch and bank. Seven feet tall in places
and 250 feet at its widest, there is an entrance/exit to the north-west and
south-east. At the circle's centre an uncremated human body was found.

THE DEVIL'S ARROWS, *Boroughbridge, North Yorkshire*
Three giant gritstone monoliths stand slightly out of alignment in a field on
the very edge of Boroughbridge, a few hundred yards from the roaring
traffic of the A1. These are the Devil's Arrows. Across the road a red brick
housing estate boasts such names as Arrow Terrace and Druids Meadow.
Each arrow is estimated to weigh over forty tons, the largest being over
twenty-two feet tall. It is believed that they were cut from a quarry six miles
away, over 2000 years ago. The top of each arrow seems to have been
grooved; the cuts were made either by weathering or, as some muse, by the
arrows' original creators – prehistoric man. Legend has it that the Devil,
angered one day, took up his crossbow and fired three bolts from his
position on Howe Hill at the village of Aldborough where there was a
Christian settlement, later to become the Roman town of Isurium. He
missed his target and the arrows fell where they have remained to this day.

AVEBURY HENGE AND STONE CIRCLE, *Avebury, Wiltshire*

Avebury henge and stone circle is the largest prehistoric monument in Europe, covering twenty-eight acres and encompassing most of the small village of Avebury. The henge was built in about 1800 BC, and is estimated to have taken one and a half million man hours to create. It is nearly a mile around its perimeter. The internal quarry ditch is thirty feet deep and, with the outer bank, is, in places, fifty feet from top to bottom. The henge originally contained three stone circles. The largest is the outer one, and this was made up of about 100 forty-ton sarsen stones. Twenty seven now remain; within this circle are the remains of two small circles. Most of these stones have disappeared, having been broken up and used for the construction of the village during the seventeenth and eighteenth centuries.

THE MERRY MAIDENS AND THE PIPERS, *Nr Lamorna, Cornwall*

This perfect circular stone temple lies in a field adjacent to the B3315 on the Newlyn to Land's End road, near the village of Lamorna. Each of the nineteen granite stones placed equidistant from the next, has been carefully shaped and graded. The tallest – four feet high – is in the south west, and the shortest directly opposite. There is a gap where a twentieth stone may once have stood; but this may simply be a space forming a natural entrance to the circle. According to legend, probably initiated by the early Christian Church to stop the pagan Cornish peasantry continuing old habits, these stones were once nineteen young maidens from a nearby village who, rather than attending church on the Sabbath, were led a dance by two evil spirits in the guise of pipers. A bolt of lightning from a clear blue sky transformed them into stone for all to see – a continual reminder of the power of the Almighty. A little to the north are two very large and tall menhirs, one hundred yards apart, known as the Pipers. One is fifteen feet tall and the other is over thirteen feet. They were excavated in 1871 and found to have been buried five feet into the ground. Before more modern farming methods and comprehensive field clearance took place, this area was noted for other megalithic monuments – Bronze Age holed stones, unfortunately now lost, possibly another circle, and burial chambers.

THE BLIND FIDDLER AND TWO SISTERS, *Nr Penzance, Cornwall*

Often missed behind high hedges just off the main road running south from Penzance to Land's End are two inscrutable Bronze Age stone monuments. The Two Sisters and the Blind Fiddler are within a quarter of a mile of each other, at Higher Drift and Catchall. Shrouded in mystery and sea mist, these menhirs are just two of Cornwall's many 'peopled' stones. Huge and enigmatic, they stand eleven feet tall. It would not be surprising if, four thousand years ago, these stones were part of the same ritual monument complex, even though they are not within sight of each other. The menhirs are said to be people turned to stone for acting in an unchristian manner; the Blind Fiddler for playing his instrument on the Sabbath, the Two Sisters for non-attendance at church.

SHOVEL DOWN STONE ROW, LONG STONE AND SCORHILL STONE CIRCLE, *Nr Chagford, Devon*

On a wild summer's evening, with the dark sunlit clouds tumbling over Stone Tor Hill, Scorhill Stone Circle (see overleaf) is truly awe-inspiring. This large and now semi-derelict stone circle comprises of about two dozen stones. Many have now fallen, others have been removed. It has been suggested from a study of the spaces that the circle might once have comprised of over forty stones. Several are sharply pointed and the tallest is over eight feet high. Others seem to have been carefully shaped, and are triangular.

A mile away to the south, across the fast-flowing North Teign River, the extensive Shovel Down Bronze Age settlement is in sight. Here there are good examples of the enigmatic stone rows that Dartmoor is famous for. There are at least two double stone rows ending in burial cists. A long single stone row leads from these up and over the hill to a ten-foot-tall menhir, known as the Long Stone. In more recent times it has been used as a parish boundary mark. Little is known of the stone rows, but they certainly appear to act as avenues leading up to burial sites. Perhaps they too once represented a path for departing spirits.

THE HURLERS, *Minions, Cornwall*

The windswept moorland village of Minions, which was once prosperous
from mining but now consists of a pub and a scattering of houses, is the
home of a Bronze Age stone temple, known to all as The Hurlers. It
consists of three large aligned stone circles, running from north-east to
south-west. The most northerly and the most southerly are perfect circles,
while the central ring is slightly egg shaped. All the stones in the central
circle have been graded to the same height; some are diamond-shaped,
others round, some bluntly pointed. One has been shaped so that its
uppermost edge is clefted. The structures are said to be Cornishmen turned
to stone for playing the ancient game of hurling on a Holy Day. An hour's
drive away to the south-west the men of St Colomb Major have been more
fortunate; though they 'Hurl the Silver Ball' annually on Shrove Tuesday,
they are still flesh and blood. According to legend it is difficult to count the
number of Hurlers at Minions, but should you do so correctly a misfortune
will befall you.

summit of Belstone Tor, the views across to the East Okement River and beyond to Scarey Tor and Cullever Steps are spectacular. Some authorities have suggested that the circle was erected around a burial mound, which now no longer exists. There are several legends associated with the circle: one is that maidens were found dancing on the Sabbath and were turned to stone for their sin; another is that the stones represent members of a witches coven; and a third is that the stones move off each noon for a drink, presumably in the East Okement River. Unfortunately, I left before midday and was unable to witness this!

STONEHENGE, *Nr Amesbury, Wiltshire*

Stonehenge is Britain's best known prehistoric monument. West of Amesbury on the busy A303, it attracts thousands of visitors each year. All come to marvel at this truly magnificent temple dedicated to the ancient gods. What many do not realize is that the Stonehenge we see today was built in three stages and took over 700 years to complete. Early mention of Stonehenge is made by the twelfth-century chronicler Geoffrey of Monmouth who claimed that it was brought by a tribe of giants from Africa to Ireland, and from there 'flown' by the wizard Merlin across the Irish Sea. Another legend is that the stones were stolen from an Irish woman by the Devil, and re-erected on Salisbury Plain by Merlin for Ambrosius Aurelianus, the King of the Britons. John Aubrey, the seventeenth-century archaeologist, claimed it to be the Temple of the Sun where Druids practised ritual magic and human sacrifice. Modern-day Druids only celebrate the rising of the midsummer sun at the site.

THE NINE STONES, *Nr Belstone, Devon*

Most commonly known as simply The Nine Stones (there are in fact sixteen or seventeen of them), though sometimes known as the Nine Maidens and at one time the Seventeen Brothers, this small and beautifully situated stone circle can easily be reached from Belstone village. From here, just below the

LONG MEG AND HER DAUGHTERS, *Nr Little Salkeld, Cumbria*

Long Meg and her Daughters is one of Britain's largest Bronze Age stone circles. This near-perfect circle is 560 feet across and originally comprised about 70 locally-quarried granite blocks. Only 57 now remain. There are signs of a bank and once this may have been a henge monument. Long Meg, unlike her Daughters, is a 12-foot-tall, shaped and pointed red sandstone outlyer, which was probably quarried 1½ miles away. She stands about fifty feet from her Daughters. On the inside, near the base, is a faint spiral carving. Like other megalithic monuments Long Meg and her Daughters represent a coven of witches turned to stone by a saint for practising their pagan craft.

STANTON DREW STONE CIRCLE, *Stanton Drew, Avon*

Stanton Drew is the second largest stone circle complex after Avebury and comprises of three circles, two avenues and a cove of three stones. The largest circle has a diameter of 340 feet and now consists of 27 stones. All the stones in this Neolithic complex are large, undressed, sandstone blocks that have been quarried from a variety of sites. As with other megalithic monuments the stones represent a party that turned into an all-night revel. As midnight approached the fiddler refused to carry on playing, saying that he could not perform on the Sabbath. The bride swore at him and vowed that she would find a replacement even if it meant going to hell. Soon afterwards an old man appeared and said he would carry on where the other fiddler had left off. They danced till dawn and by all accounts it was a wild and frenzied party. At first light the bride discovered that the old man was the Devil and, when the villagers woke, they found that the wedding party had been turned to stone. As the Devil left, his final words were that he would play once more but until he does the wedding party will stand cold in a field by the river. The three stones known as the Cove are said to represent the bride, groom, and parson. The name of the village and circle derives from *stan* meaning stone and Drew from the thirteenth-century family that once farmed this land.

MITCHELLS FOLD STONE CIRCLE, *Nr Chirbury,* *Shropshire*

Mitchells Fold Stone Circle is Early Bronze Age, between 2000 BC and 1200 BC. Fifteen stones are all that remain. Once there were twice that many, and perhaps a central stone. The construction is nearly perfectly circular, but with a noticable flattening on the southern side which could have been deliberate, and is small enough to have been constructed by a single Bronze Age family or a small community group. All the stones come from the nearby Stapley Hill. According to legend, a giant cow used to live on the moor and would give milk to anyone who visited. One day a witch milked her into a sieve and the cow disappeared. The witch was turned to stone and a circle put up to keep her in. The story is told, carved on a capital of the Holy Trinity Church in Middleton-in-Chirbury by the Rev. Waldegrave Brewster in 1879.

MEN-AN-TOL, *Nr Morvah, Cornwall*

The Men-an-Tol, or 'Holed Stone', consists of four or five stones, including one that has now fallen. It lies a mile off the Morvah to Madron road on Penwith Moor. It is considered to be a Bronze Age construction, between 4000 and 2500 years old. Holed stones can be found at various locations over the British Isles and in Europe and, according to some authorities, they were usually sited at places with high amounts of the earth's energy. Placed near stone rings and used in conjunction with standing stones, they were thought to have magic curative powers and were also associated with fertility rites. Until recently babies and young children were passed naked through the 'female' holed stone three times, and then pulled across the grass against the sun three more times, while adults had to crawl around and then through the stone nine times for the magic powers to work.

THE TOLVAN HOLED STONE, *Nr Gweek, Cornwall*

The Tolvan Holed Stone stands in the back garden of a cottage at Tolvan Cross, a mile north of the creekside village of Gweek. Possibly Bronze Age, this most unusual and enigmatic monolith is just over seven feet tall, and wider at the base. It is unknown how far into the ground it stands. The circular hole is seventeen inches in diameter, and like the other holed stones in Penwith its edge is bevelled as if some Bronze Age rope had worn the granite smooth with rubbing. Holed stones are a complete mystery, but are now generally credited with having healing powers. This one is said to ensure fertility, particularly to newly married couples, but only after they have squeezed their naked bodies through it.

THE HOLED STONES, *Nr Tregeseal, Cornwall*

The spirits of the ancients – 'The Little People' – are still said to be active around the demonic-shaped Carn Kenidjack (meaning head of a flying serpent). Lying in a bed of purple heather, peppered with yellow gorse, just below the Carn, lie four, small but most mysterious holed, granite stones (one has now fallen and broken). The stones are in a west-east alignment and were first noted and drawn in the mid-nineteenth century. Associated with them are two more holed stones – outlyers. One is very similar and has the correct bevelled edge, while the sixth has a sharp drilled feel to it and must therefore be regarded with suspicion. The alignment lies within the remains of a Bronze Age settlement. Nearby are hut circles and several barrows, two known as The Giants Graves. The Tregeseal Nine Maidens Stone Circle is only a short walk away.

DOD LAW ROCK CARVINGS, *Nr Doddington, Northumberland*

High on windswept Doddington Moor, past Wooler Golf Club and over the ninth green, but before the Shepherd's Cottage, is the most interesting inscribed stone slab on the moor. A large, flat rock has been incised with numerous 'cup' marks; these have been grouped together and surrounded with crude rectangles and double circles ('ring' marks). All seem to be linked together by linear markings. Near the Iron Age hillfort on slightly higher ground, other examples of incised rocks can be found. The area once had a stone circle and barrows, all of which have now vanished.

ROUGHTING LINN INSCRIBED STONES, *Nr Doddington, Northumberland*

Many consider these 'cup' and 'ring' marks to be some of the best examples in northern England. Found in a wood on Roughting Linn farm, adjacent to a minor road leading from Kimmerston to Barmoor, and within the shadow of Goatcragg Hill, these enigmatic Bronze Age inscriptions have never been fully explained. They are most usually found on near-horizontal rocky outcrops, and often near Iron Age forts. Some theories suggest that they are Bronze Age games, representations of the sun, moon and stars, ways of measuring light and time, maps of religious sites or moulds for making metal rings. Occasionally found in burial tombs and on monoliths, these markings are most commonly found in northern England and southern Scotland.

LORDINSHAW HILL CUP AND RING MARKS,
Nr Rothbury, Northumberland

Here is an example of a rock inscribed with 'cup' and 'ring' marks. It can be found off a very minor road leading into Rothbury Forest, two miles south of the market town of Rothbury, near an Iron Age hill fort with spectacular views across open countryside.

MAIDENS CASTLE, *Dorchester, Dorset*

The outer perimeter ramparts of Maidens Castle measure approximately one and a half miles and encompass an area of 120 acres. This huge hillfort started out as a Neolithic causeway camp in about 3000 BC. In the late Neolithic period a massive longbarrow, over 1700 feet in length, was constructed. The camp was then abandoned. Maidens Castle became an important Iron Age centre between 350 BC and 70 BC. Massive triple and double ramparts were constructed as well as complex entrances. Little is known of life here during this period but the inhabitants were eventually beaten by the Roman Vespasian second legion in AD 43. The Britons were allowed to stay for a while before the camp was finally moved to the new Roman town of Durnovaria, which became known as Dorchester.

LABYRINTH ROCK CARVINGS, *Nr Tintagel, Cornwall*

A few miles away from the summer madding crowds of Tintagel, on the B3263 heading north towards Boscastle, are two Bronze Age labyrinth rock carvings. Each is about one foot across, three feet apart and two feet off the ground. They are still very detailed and are incised on a sheltered slate rock face that weeps after heavy rain. They are near the bottom of 'Rocky Valley', behind a ruined mill, off a steep winding overhung path leading to the sea. Both labyrinths are Cretan in design, which has led some authorities to speculate that they are not in fact Bronze Age, but more recent. Labyrinthine and spiral carvings can be found in prehistoric caves and burial chambers in many parts of the world. It has been suggested that this type of carving symbolizes prehistoric man's soul journeying from death to eventual rebirth.

CARN EUNY FOGOU, *Nr Sancreed, Cornwall*

At the end of a lane running west out of the hamlet of Brane, after a short walk over well-signposted fields, Carn Euny Iron Age village can be found. Signs of both Neolithic and Bronze Age activity have been found here, but this is primarily an Iron Age site. Around 200 BC, wooden huts were erected by the farming and livestock-breeding community, and by the first century AD stone buildings were being used. These early Cornishmen built an underground passage, known as a fogou, and off this, at Carn Euny, is a unique circular corbelled chamber, reached via a 'creep' passage. No one knows the mysteries of this perfect souterrain. It has been suggested that it could have been used for storage, habitation or for purposes of ritual.

GRIMSPOUND, *Nr Widecombe in the Moor, Devon*

Wild and windy now, but much milder in the Bronze Age, this farming settlement at Hookney Tor is easily accessible as it is only a few hundred yards off the Widecombe in the Moor to Lettaford road. Probably dating from 1000 BC, Grimspound now comprises of twenty-seven hut circles and some cattle shelters. About four acres are encompassed by a dry stone wall, which was once nine feet thick and five feet high. Clearly not a defensive device, this enclosure was for keeping cattle in and wild animals out. A stream runs through the area, and on the upper slope there is a paved entrance. Grimspound is named after the mythical Anglo-Saxon figure Grim, God of Battle, Master of Fury and Leader of the Wild Hunt. Sherlock Holmes had Watson bivouac in one of the hut circles during his investigations in *The Hound of the Baskervilles*.

WADE'S CAUSEWAY, *Nr Goathland, North Yorkshire*

Known locally as Wade's Causeway, this is the longest and best preserved
section of Roman road in Britain. It runs across wild and open moorland for
one and a quarter miles south of Goathland. The sixteen-foot-wide road,
with a slightly raised centre, for good drainage, has had its top surface
eroded away. What are left are the foundation setts. According to legend a
giant named Wade and his equally large wife Bell lived in nearby Mulgrave.
Each day she had to cross Wheeldale Moor to milk her cow. Wheeldale
Moor is a boggy, windy and wild place, and even for a giantess it could be
dangerous. She asked Wade if they could build a pathway to make her daily
journey safer. He agreed and they both set to work. She collected sand and
gravel from Sandsend, while he dug out larger rocks from the Hole of
Horcum. After they had died the path fell into disuse and was eventually
covered over again by the moor.

ROB OF RISINGHAM, *West Woodburn, Northumberland*

According to legend, Rob of Risingham was one of two giant brothers who
quarrelled over hunting rights. Ella (who gives his name to the ancient
village of Elsdon some eight miles away) was the weaker of the two and Rob
managed to poison him. All that now remains of Rob is his lower half,
carved on a rock down a track behind Cragg Quarry, on the edge of the
village of West Woodburn. One of only a few Roman carvings left in situ,
this local 'god of the forest' must have been adopted by some men at the
Roman garrison town of Habitancum. He carries a hare in one hand and a
bow in the other, and wears a Roman tunic. For many years the carving was
complete in the rock face but apparently towards the end of the nineteenth
century the popularity of Rob of Risingham was so great that the landowner
became fed up with the constant flow of visiting tourists. He took it upon
himself to destroy the legend by blowing Rob up. This act of vandalism so
enraged the villagers that they ostracized the landowner and eventually
forced him to leave the area.

THE LONG MAN OF WILMINGTON, *Nr Wilmington, East Sussex*

The Long Man of Wilmington is the largest representation of the human figure in western Europe. It stands on the steep, north-facing, chalk slopes of Windover Hill, part of the Sussex Downs, and is over two hundred and thirty feet tall. The Long Man has in the past been known as the Lone Man, and also the Lanky Man. This tall athletic figure stands with his arms outstretched, and is first mentioned by Burrell in 1779, where he is shown to be carrying a rake and scythe. The present depiction dates from 1873 when the Duke of Devonshire, whose land he stood on, gave instructions for the figure to be restored and outlined in yellow bricks. There are numerous theories and legends as to the Long Man's origin. One tells of two giants who fought. The Wilmington giant was killed and lies where he fell. Another theory is that it is the work of the Benedictine monks of Wilmington Priory who, in the early part of the fifteenth century, made the figure as some kind of landmark. Another is that it is the work of Roman soldiers who cut the figure in a classical pose. A similar figure – that of Denarius of Vetranius – can be found on seventh-century Roman coins. Another theory is that it is a Saxon farmer with his rake and scythe, and yet another that it is a Saxon warrior-god with his spears; a similar figure has been found on a bronze buckle in a seventh-century grave at Finglesham, Kent.

THE CERNE GIANT, *Cerne Abbas, Dorset*

The Cerne Giant is a huge and impressive figure cut into the hillside near Cerne Abbas. He is one hundred and eighty feet from head to toe, and forty feet across his shoulders. In his right hand he carries an enormous 120-foot club. But his most famous and prominent feature is his erect phallus, which has led to a variety of fertility superstitions. Barren women were said to conceive soon after sleeping on the Giant's naked body, while young women wishing to keep their lovers faithful would walk around the figure three times. No one knows exactly when or who first cut the figure. The first written reference is by Hutchins in his *Guide to Dorset*, 1751. The figure is described as being cut in 1539 and representing the loathsome Abbot Thomas Corton, who was eventually expelled from the area. The Giant has also been seen as representing variously the Roman hunter god Hercules, a Saxon prince, and the Celtic god Noden. Archaeologists using resistivity tests have recently discovered that he once carried an animal skin in his left hand, which supports the Hercules theory.

OFFA'S DYKE, *Nr Knighton, Hereford and Worcester*

Offa's Dyke stretches from the Wye Valley in the south to the Dee Valley in the north, and now roughly follows the boundary between England and Wales. Constructed by Offa, who reigned from 757–96 AD, to act as a statement of ownership and a boundary line between his powerful and prosperous kingdom of Mercia to the east and the troublesome Welsh tribes to the west, Offa's Dyke can still be seen clearly for over seventy miles. Built in peacetime, it was too huge and long to be defended. After twelve centuries it is still, in places, over fifty feet from the bottom of the westerly ditch to the top of the ramparts. Little is known of Offa's reign save that he ruled much of England from the English Channel to the Humber. He called himself 'The King of the English' and 'Emperor'. During his reign the first silver pennies were introduced. These were dated and bore his portrait.

THE DEVIL'S DYKE, *Nr Newmarket, Cambridgeshire*

After Offa's Dyke, the Devil's Dyke is the largest and longest manmade earth obstruction in Britain. The dyke is of uncertain age but is thought to pre-date late Saxon times. Archaeologists have now established that it was only in use for three years. It has been found mentioned as a landmark in sixth-and seventh-century manuscripts. Built either as a defence during a period of warfare between various Saxon tribes and Britons, or else constructed as a defence for East Anglia from the powerful kingdom of Mercia, it is very close to Fleam Dyke and Pamisford and Heydon Ditches. It is seven miles long, running north-west to south-east between Reach and Woodditton, cutting through Newmarket Heath.

DOZMARY POOL, *Nr Bolventor, Cornwall*

Striking south down a minor road nearly opposite the now sadly over-commercialized Jamaica Inn at Bolventor, made famous by Daphne Du Maurier, you can drive up onto Bodmin Moor which still retains its windswept beauty. Dark, awesome and mysterious, the 'bottomless' Dozmary Pool on the moor is, according to legend, one of the places where the Knight St Bedivere, while carrying the mortally wounded King Arthur back from his last battle at Camlann, twice failed to throw the bejewelled

sword Excalibur into the lake. When eventually he did, according to folklore, it was caught by the Lady of the Lake, who held it aloft before disappearing with it for ever. Jan Tregeagle, the murderous Cornishman, was made to drain this 'bottomless' pool with a broken limpet shell as a punishment, before fleeing to Roche's Rock (see opposite). Across the water is the site of a Bronze Age flint factory. While I was there, just after a rain storm, two flint arrow heads and a scraper were found by a collector.

ROCHE'S ROCK, *Roche, Cornwall*

This fourteenth-century hermitage clinging perilously to the granite outcrop on the edge of Goss Moor is thought to have been the last resting place of a leper, kept alive by his daughter who brought him food and water each day. The Hermitage is also associated with the folktale of a Cornish scoundrel, Jan Tregeagle, who amongst other things murdered a succession of his wives and children, so that he might amass a fortune. Once convicted, he was sentenced to drain the fabled bottomless Dozmary Pool with a leaky limpet shell. Tortured with the impossibility of the task, one stormy night he managed to escape across Bodmin Moor pursued by a pack of headless hounds. On reaching the Hermitage he thrust his head through the open window to reach the sanctuary of the chapel, but his body remained outside, exposed to the hounds' fury. After two days the hermit could no longer bear to hear the terrible screaming and called two saints who took Tregeagle away to Padstow Beach where he was confined and ordered to weave rope with sand for the rest of his life.

GLASTONBURY TOR, *Glastonbury, Somerset*

Improbably conical, Glastonbury Tor stands out above the Somerset levels. Considered by many New Ageists to be a spiritual home, equally as important as Avebury, Stonehenge or Silbury Hill, the tor was once an island, and as such deemed to be sacred by the pagan Celts. It is thought to have been the mysterious Isle of Avalon, in Celtic folklore a meeting place for the dead; and Gwyn-ap-nudd a Celtic god of the underworld was said to have made his kingdom Annwn here. It was here in Arthurian legend that the dying King was brought on a barge accompanied by weeping fairies. A spiral path leads up to the summit and the ruins of a church built on the site of an earlier chapel, destroyed in an earthquake. The church is dedicated to St Michael – soldier of God and victor over paganism.

ROYSTON CAVE, *Royston, Hertfordshire*

Royston Cave is under Melbourn Street, near Royston Cross, which marks the junction of Icknield Way and Ermine Street. It is believed that the Holy Cross was erected by a certain Lady Roisia, who lived in the area shortly after the Norman Conquest. The cave was possibly the oratory of a hermit, and Lady Roisia his patron. If so, he was probably the cave's sculptor. Royston Cave was discovered by workmen in 1742 and unfortunately all the excavated rubble that filled the cave was thrown away as they searched for a treasure believed to be at the bottom of the cave. None was found. The Cave is bell-shaped and carved out of solid chalk. It is thirty feet high and has a diameter of twenty feet. The carvings are of St Laurence who was martyred by being roasted on a metal grill, and St Katherine who was martyred on a spiked wheel. It is thought that John and Mary are the figures by the Crucifixion. Other saints are marked with a cross, and those who were martyred are marked with a heart. The other figures are a mystery.

ST PIRANS CROSS, *Nr Perranporth, Cornwall*

St Pirans Cross marks the place on Penhale Sands, a few miles north of the summer seaside resort of Perranporth, where according to legend the ninth-century Celtic saint St Piran landed, having sailed from Ireland 'on a mill stone'. It is one of only two three-holed Celtic crosses in Cornwall.

St Piran set up an oratory inland, and it became Perranzabuloe – derived from Piran combined with the Latin word *sabulo*, meaning 'in the sand'. The church was eventually covered by sand and was moved a quarter of a mile to the other side of a small stream, near a cross that had acted as a landmark for over two centuries. According to folklore, Penhale Sands covers the now-lost mining town of Langarroc, which once boasted seven churches. The people were blasphemous and immoral and, in an act of retribution, a great storm which was to last three days and nights completely covered the town and its people. On a stormy night it is still possible to hear the cries for help and the church bells clanging above the roar of the wind and sea.

CELTIC FACE, *Perranzabuloe, Cornwall*

This Celtic face cut into the stonework on the south-facing porch of the third St Pirans church was brought from the second church now buried on Penhale Sands. Prior to that it had adorned St Pirans ninth-century oratory.

FONT AT ST GERMOE CHURCH, *Germoe, Cornwall*

In pre-Christian Britain, the Celts venerated the human head. Not simply proof of victory over a foe, they believed that its possession would give them the power of knowledge. The Celts also venerated water, a life-giving force. Water from holy wells drunk out of a human skull was often considered more potent, and until recently this belief was still in practice at St Teilo's Well, Crinlow, Dyfed. Some holy wells are decorated with carvings of heads such as at St Ambrews Well in Cornwall. Celtic Christian baptisms took place in holy wells, and later in stone fonts positioned on the ground. The washing of feet was part of the baptism ritual. Very early fonts were often decorated with carved heads, and it seems most likely that these decorations represent the Celtic symbol of success and knowledge derived from the Cult of the Head. The ancient font at St Germoe is considered to have come from the first St Germoe Church founded by the Irish king and missionary Germochus who founded a baptistry here probably in the sixth century.

ST CLETHER'S HOLY WELL AND CHAPEL, *St Clether, Cornwall*

St Clether is not easy to find amongst the deep Cornish lanes on the edge of Bodmin Moor. Even more difficult to find is St Clether's Church, hidden behind a tall screen of trees. The Holy Well and Chapel are set some way behind the church, below a rock face. To get there, beat your way through chest-high bracken and you will emerge to find a tranquil and beautiful sanctuary. The Well is full of clear spring water, which still passes into the chapel, directly under the altar, where the once-pagan water was sanctified when the body of St Clether was lain in it. St Clether was a fourth-century Welshman who educated, baptized and conducted the funerals of the pagan Cornish. His oratory and cell were once where the chapel stands today. It was simple, there were no seats or benches, and the old and infirm would 'go to the wall', a saying still in use today. After Clether's death, the title Saint was conferred upon him, as was the custom, for founding his church.

SHEELA-NA-GIGS

Found on only a few churches in Britain, and now often unrecognizable due to weathering, these ancient carvings of a naked female displaying her genitals are thought to represent the Celtic goddess of fertility and destruction. They have been given the name Sheela-na-gig. According to legend this Celtic goddess appears to any future king as a lecherous hag, and tries to seduce him. On succeeding, she turns into a beautiful woman and gives her blessing to the success of his reign and tribe.

   The best known example of a Sheela-na-gig is carved onto a corbel of the parish church at Kilpeck (see overleaf). This and other carvings are twelfth-century. Another Sheela-na-gig appears above the priest's door of All Saints Church, Buckland (right). This Church was founded in the thirteenth century, and was extensively rebuilt in the Victorian era, when the carving might well have been repositioned. At Saint Mary and All Saints, Willingham, on the fourteenth-century rood screen, a small but beautifully preserved fantasy figure (opposite) has been carved. Described as an 'imp' this evil spirit sits with its legs wide apart, its hands stretching its mouth wide open, and an enormous tongue hanging down to its nether regions.

St Mary and St David's Church, *Kilpeck, Hereford and Worcester*

Kilpeck derives its name from the English word Kil or Cell, and Pedic or Pedoric, i.e. the Cell of St Pedic. There has been a church here since at least 650 AD and some of the Saxon remains have been incorporated into the twelfth-century church built by Hugh of Kilpeck. The Church of St Mary and St David is famous for its carvings, which today still show a remarkable amount of detail. The carvings by the so called Hereford School of craftsmen over the south doorway are undoubtedly the prize of this ancient church. Here amongst the carvings of human heads are various beasts, birds and serpents, as well as a tree of life. At the top of the right hand jamb is a Green Man figure, said to be eating the 'forbidden fruit of the tree of knowledge'.

GREEN MAN AND DRAGON BENCH ENDS, *Crowcombe, Somerset*

This beautiful church of the Holy Ghost has a remarkable display of pre-Reformation pews, one bearing the date 1534. Each bench end is superbly carved. Rural scenes and ecclesiastical events are most common, but there are also some fine examples of Green Men. He appears three times, with grapevines sprouting from his mouth. Another Green Man is horned, while another bench end shows a double headed dragon being slain. A second dragon in the bottom left hand corner has, like the Green Man figure, grapevines sprouting from its mouth. In Christian iconography the vine is a symbol of fecundity and the dragon a symbol of evil.

GREEN MAN, *Sampford Courtenay, Devon (overleaf)*

In the chancel above the altar of the parish church of St Andrew is a wood-carved Green Man. Green Man carvings can be found in numerous medieval churches throughout Britain. These mysterious carved heads have never been fully understood. A common feature of Green Men is that their heads have no bodies and foliage always sprouts from their mouths. The most common explanation is that they are synonymous with the Jack in Green of May celebrations – a man peering through greenery, still to be found on village pub signs. But before the church renamed this pagan deity Jack, or Robin Goodfellow, he had been a Celtic horned god of fertility venerated since pre-Christian times with processions of young girls and dancing.

THE RUDSTON MONOLITH, *Rudston, Humberside*

Standing in the graveyard of All Saints Church, Rudston, is Britain's largest monolith – 25 feet 9 inches tall – looking out of place and not unlike a huge gravestone with a lead cap on. Made from gritstone and transported from Clayton Bay ten miles away, this carefully shaped rock was once used by Late Neolithic and Early Bronze Age man in ritual ceremonies. At the north-east corner of the graveyard is a companion stone measuring about three feet tall. The early Christians who built All Saints chose this already sacred and venerated pagan site, so to engulf those beliefs and 'baptize' the stone. Early Christian missionaries possibly attached a wooden cross to it. The name Rudston derives from the old English words *rood* or cross, and *stan* meaning stone. A common justification for the close proximity of the stone to the church is that the Devil, angered by the builders, hurled the javelin-shaped rock at the church. It missed and the stone landed where it stands today.

THE MERMAID'S CHAIR, *Zennor, Cornwall*

Saint Senara founded the church at Zennor over a thousand years ago and the Zennor Mermaid is carved onto the side of a short wooden bench in the church, known as the Mermaid's Chair. It is probably about five or six hundred years old. In one hand she carries a mirror and in the other a comb. She is the symbol of Aphrodite – the goddess of love and beauty, who came from the sea. Folklore tells us of a beautiful young maiden who regularly sat at the back of the church to listen to the choir practise. The squire's son, Mathew Trewhella, had a pure and distinctive voice, and she was overcome. One evening she managed to lure him to the stream that flows through the village, and from there they went together to the sea at Pendover Cove (now called Mermaid's Cove). He was never to return, but on a clear summer evening it is possible to hear the lovers singing together from beneath the waves.

KNOWLTON HENGE CIRCLE, *Nr Gussage All Saints, Dorset*

Knowlton Henge is now all that is clearly visible of a triple Neolithic henge construction, situated just off the B3078, and down a minor road leading to Gussage All Saints, in a beautiful and unspoilt part of Dorset. The three henges get progressively larger. The smallest is to the north. The central henge is over three hundred feet across, and has banks that are eleven feet high in places. The internal quarry ditch reaches up to thirty feet across. There is an entrance exit to the south-west–north-east. The largest henge is the most southerly, but this has now been almost completely ploughed out, and is bisected by the B3078. Undoubtedly the central henge was preserved only because of the building of the original twelfth-century, now ruinous, church, which was designed within this pagan and ritual meeting place.

NINE MENS MORRIS, *Finchingfield, Essex*

Carved on to the window sill of St John the Baptist Church is the ancient board game, Nine Mens Morris. The board is made up of three concentric squares. It is played by two people, with nine counters each, the object being to get three counters in a row and to capture all opposing pieces. The game has been carved onto the steps of the Accropolis in Athens, on the deck of a Viking ship in Norway, and on a Roman tile dug up in Silchester. It is known and played in the Amazon, India and China. In France it is called

marelle, which is similar to the French word for hopscotch; according to some this game derives from maze games, which in turn derive from an early Christian belief in the penitential symbolism of the maze, seen as the journey of a lost soul. In Greece it is called petteia, after Palamedes who invented the game before the siege of Troy.

Shakespeare wrote in *A Midsummer Night's Dream*:
'The Nine Mens Morris is fill'd up with mud,
And the quaint mazes in the wanton green
For lack of tread are indistinguishable.'

JULIAN BOWER, *Alkborough, Humberside*

Julian Bower, the turf maze overlooking the River Trent and Humber estuary, is a short walk along Back Street from the village church, where an exact copy was cut into the flagstone floor of the porch during the restoration in 1887. The maze is thought to be thirteenth-century and made by monks from a nearby monastery, possibly for penitential purposes. First mentioned in the seventeenth century by Abraham de la Pryme who called it 'Gillians Bore . . . nothing but a great labarinth cut into the ground', the maze was during these times used for village games and sports. Legend tells of a river spirit called Gur who was so disenchanted with the Christian visitors to the maze that he vowed to destroy it. He created a mighty tidal wave that washed up the River Trent. Fortunately it was not strong enough and Julian Bower survived. Gur still lives and each spring he tries again by sending another tidal wave racing up the river past Alkborough. It is now called the Trent Bore.

CAVENDISH MEMORIAL, *Edensor, Derbyshire*

The sixth Duke of Devonshire undertook monumental alterations to Chatsworth. One of them was the moving of the village of Edensor (the village nearest the house), and positioning it out of view. In 1867 a replacement church was built, which incorporated some features from the original church, including the massive monument to Henry Cavendish who died in 1611 and his younger brother William, sons of Bess of Hardwick. They both now lie head to toe. Henry is portrayed as a full-length skeleton while his younger brother is shown in a shroud.

Henry's epitaph reads:

He was not merely the best man of his own, but of every age, nor can his character be suppressed or spoken of without difficulty, he claimed no honors and yet obtained all.

SIR ROGER ROCKLEY'S TOMB, *Worsbrough, South Yorkshire*

The two-tier memento mori of Sir Roger Rockley in St Mary's parish church is, considering its age, in remarkable condition. Carved in oak, and then covered in fine linen, it still carries the original paint. Sir Roger Rockley died in 1535 shortly after his father from whom he inherited the title. He died in his late twenties, having been married twice and having fathered four children. He was a popular man and in his will, dated eleven years before his death, he made provision for a hat, a brass pot and five shillings to every maiden married in Worsbrough for seven years after his death, and to single men three shillings. He also provided for hospitality for travellers and villagers for fifteen years after his death. According to Dodsworth a local historian who wrote a History of Yorkshire in 1619, inscribed below the cadaver was the epitaph, 'I beget children daily and I am unrepentant'. This epitaph was removed, probably during Victorian times, for fear of offending.

ROOD SCREEN CARVINGS, *Sancreed, Cornwall*

Carved onto the sixteenth-century rood screen at Sancreed parish church are many 'grotesques', a janiform head of a woman and a triple-faced carving of a king. In Celtic mythology the head was considered to be a symbol of power, knowledge and divine persona. Many Celtic gods had three heads, and a few were given two, the deity's power multiplying according to the number of heads he or she had. These many-faced gods were central to the Celtic understanding of life. The three-faced king has parallels with the Christian concept of the Trinity – God the Father, God the Son and God the Holy Spirit. The woman's head may represent a Celtic deity with the power to look forward into the future and back into the past at the same time.

THE DEVIL'S STONE, *Copgrove, North Yorkshire*

Over the centuries many superstitions have grown up around the church, which has in the past played a much greater role in people's lives than it does today. One such superstition was that the north side of the church belonged to the Devil. At St Michael and All Angels Church during restoration in the nineteenth century, the so-called 'Devil's Stone' was removed from the north chancel wall and repositioned on the exterior north-east corner of the church. This carved stone is probably of Roman-British origin and represents one of the Celtic deities. A similar figure can be found in Maryport, Cumbria. In northern England this deity was often shown horned and naked, and represents a god of fertility who was also a hunter god – a defender of his people.

THE ROUND HOUSES, *Veryan, Cornwall*

Veryan has five Round Houses; two pairs at either end of the village (one on the Pendower Road, the other at Tollyfrank) and a fifth house behind the village school. They were built by the Reverend Jeremiah Trist for his daughters, though when he built the houses he only had three. The houses are of cob construction on stone foundations, and, at the time of building, were considered easy to maintain. They are copies of a house his friend Charles Penrose had built at Ethy in St Winnow in 1811. All are now in private ownership and have been converted. Legend tells that they were built round so that the Devil had no corners to hide in, and that they were topped off with a cross to prevent him entering the village.

BRIMHAM ROCKS, *Nr Pateley Bridge, North Yorkshire*

Perched on an escarpment above Nidderdale in the Vale of York, off the main road running from Pateley Bridge to Summer Bridge, these weird and spectacular rocks loom up from the bleak windswept Brimham Moor and cover over fifty acres. In the eighteenth century Brimham Rocks were thought to have been created by Druids for their ritual gatherings and were given such names as The Druid's Writing Desk, Lovers Leap, Watch Dog and the Druid's Cave. The rock formations are in fact natural and consist of millstone grit fashioned by the wind and the rain.

THE CHEESEWIRING AND DRUIDS CHAIR, *Nr Minions, Cornwall*

On the eastern edge of Bodmin Moor and only a short distance from the Hurlers are the massive, naturally weathered Cheesewiring and Druids Chair. Both are natural rock formations, but in the past were often considered to have been made by the Druids. According to folklore a Druid who once lived here owned a magic golden cup that, mysteriously, never ran dry. Travellers were always rewarded with refreshment. One day a rider swore he would drink the cup dry. Unable to do so, he became furious and rode off with it. In his rage his horse fell and he died. The golden cup was buried with him. During excavations of a nearby cist in 1818 a skeleton and a golden cup were found. The cup, known as the Rillaton Cup, dates from 1500 BC and can now be seen in the British Museum.

BOWERMAN'S NOSE, *Nr Manaton, Devon*

This forty-foot-high, much loved Dartmoor landmark resembles a giant with a large bulbous nose. Standing high on a rocky outcrop near Hound Tor on Hayne Down, and once thought to have been worshipped by the Druids, this entirely natural, granite, weathered sculpture looks at certain angles not dissimilar to the mysterious sculptures on Easter Island. Legend tells how the Hunter of the Moor, known as Bowerman, was turned into stone with his pack of hounds for hunting down a hare which turned out to be a witch in disguise. Etymologists tell us, however, that 'bowerman' is more likely a corruption of the Celtic *vedr maen* meaning great stone.

ROBIN HOOD'S STRIDE, *Birchover, Derbyshire*

These two tors are known to rock climbers as the Weasel and Inaccessible, but are most commonly called Robin Hood's Stride. They are eighteen feet tall and twenty-two yards apart. They stand on a rocky outcrop known as the Mock Beggars Hall (because it has two 'chimneys'), near an ancient track called the Portway, numerous ancient barrows and, at one time, several stone circles. The tors are a curious pair of Druidical monuments and in prehistory no doubt played a part in cult worship. They are faintly marked with Bronze Age 'cup' and 'ring' marks. Legend has it that this Robin Hood is not the one of Nottingham fame, but a giant Green Man who urinated into the meadow below while standing with a foot on each 'chimney'. The Seven Maidens who witnessed this act were turned into stone and are called The Grey Ladies.

their cosmic intentions in regard to mankind'. The folly was built, true to tradition, in an oak grove about five miles away from Swinton Hall, but the grove was unfortunately cut down during the 1914–18 war. The folly now stands in the centre of an evergreen plantation off the Ilton to Healey road, west of Masham.

QUINTA STONEHENGE, *Nr Weston Rhyn, Shropshire*
Frederick Richard West M.P. sold Quinta House and his three-thousand-acre estate in 1854. But before doing so he had become interested, like other Victorian gentlemen, in improving the look of his parkland. West, like Danby, had undoubtedly seen Stonehenge, and rather than building a foreign temple or ruin, as was the fashion, he decided on what he believed was a Celtic temple. His reinforced concrete Stonehenge was built on specially raised ground in a corner of a field by a wood. It could not be seen from the road, or from Quinta House, except from second floor bedroom and apartment windows. It is thought that it was constructed for the enjoyment of West's wife, Maria. Quinta House is now an Evangelical Centre.

ILTON DRUIDS FOLLY, *Nr Masham, North Yorkshire*
Ilton Druids Folly, a miniature Stonehenge on Ilton Moor, was created by William Danby, the cultured and generous squire of Swinton Hall, following his return from a tour of Europe in 1790. During his travels he had become intrigued with the Cult of the Druids, and by 1800 his perfect replica of a Druidical temple was complete. It was said that he would 'retire from the world and meditate upon the esoteric meaning of their [Druids'] rites and

THE METHODIST CATHEDRAL, *Gwennap, Cornwall*

About one thousand years after the last of many saints were to visit and leave their names inscribed on churches and in villages throughout Cornwall, another evangelist preacher made his way there. John Wesley was the fifteenth child of Revd. Samuel and Susanna Wesley. Born in 1703 he became the leader of a group of Christian undergraduates while at Oxford. They were nicknamed the 'method-ists' because of their methodical way of

living. Amongst the mining community in Cornwall, Wesley found a receptive audience. He first preached at Gwennap in 1743, but it was not until a storm in 1762, when he and his congregation were forced to seek shelter, that he found the 'methodist cathedral'. He described it as a 'green hollow gently shelving down about fifty feet deep'. It had in fact been used as a cock pit until then. In 1806 it was remodelled and can now hold as many as a thousand worshippers.

MOW COP SHAM CASTLE, *Mow Cop, Cheshire*

Mow Cop means 'lofty and exposed summit' and that name was given to the sham castle that stands on the peak of an isolated outcrop of millstone grit, over a thousand feet above sea level, near the small industrial town of Congleton. It was built in 1754 by the brothers John and Ralph Harding for Randle Wilbraham of Rode Hall, three miles away. Originally designed as a two-storey summer house, it was shared with the Wilbrahams' neighbours, the Sneyds of Keele, who owned the Staffordshire side of the property. In the nineteenth century Mow Cop achieved some fame as the meeting place for the breakaway Methodists known as Ranters, later called Primitive Methodists. Open air 'camp meetings' were held here. At the centenary of their first open air meeting in 1907, over one hundred thousand people are said to have gathered for an open air service.

CHERHILL WHITE HORSE, *Cherhill, Wiltshire*

The Cherhill Horse is also known as the Oldbury Horse, as it lies on Cherhill Down immediately below Oldbury Castle. It was designed in 1780 by 'Mad' Dr Christopher Alsop – 'mad' because he had an unusual interest in white horses. He was apparently impressed by the work carried out by Mr Gee, steward to Lord Abingdon, who had recently decided to redesign the original Westbury Horse (right). The Horse was pegged out with white flags following instructions shouted into a megaphone by Dr Alsop from over a mile away, so that he could get the foreshortening correct. The Horse is over 140 feet long. The eye was originally made with bottle bottoms which glittered in the sunlight but unfortunately this was vandalized in the nineteenth century.

WESTBURY WHITE HORSE, *Westbury, Wiltshire*

The Westbury White Horse is the best known of the Wiltshire White Horses, measuring 175 feet from head to tail, and standing 107 feet tall. It stands below the Iron Age fort of Bratton on a steep chalk slope and can be seen for miles around. The present Horse was designed by Lord Abingdon's steward, Mr Gee, in 1778; he incorporated a smaller and much older horse into his new design. The original horse is said to date from the ninth century and was carved to celebrate Alfred the Great's victorious Battle of Ethandun in AD 878 which was to end Danish desires to conquer Britain.

THE WATLINGTON WHITE MARK, *Watlington, Oxfordshire*

The Watlington White Mark was originally designed by local squire Edward Horne, who felt that the Norman church of St Leonard, when viewed from his home, would appear more impressive if it looked as if it had a spire. He had this unusual folly cut into the chalk of Watlington Hill in 1764. It is 270 feet tall and 36 feet wide.

THE SUGAR LOAF, *Brightling, East Sussex*

Folly-building was 'Mad' Jack Fuller's penchant and, besides the pyramid he built as his mausoleum, he constructed five other follies on his estate. The Sugar Loaf, according to legend, was erected overnight so that he might win a wager. While in London he had bet with some friends over dinner that he could see the spire of St Giles Church in Dallington from his estate in Brightling. On his return to the country he discovered that he could not, and so set about designing and constructing his own to look like the Dallington church spire. Known as the Sugar Loaf it was probably erected between 1810 and 1820 and sits in what used to be known as Towerfields, just off the Battle to Heathfield road, at Woods Corner. It is 35 feet tall and was once lived in.

MAD JACK FULLER'S PYRAMID, *Brightling, East Sussex*

'Mad Jack' Fuller was born in 1757, educated at Eton, and inherited the family fortune and estates on his twentieth birthday. He was a staunch Conservative and Member of Parliament for Lewes. His outspokenness, antics and loud bellowing voice earned him the nickname 'Mad Jack'. Later in life his twenty-two-stone frame caused him to be known as the Hippopotamus. He spent many years designing a series of follies for his country estate at Brightling, where he was buried when he died aged seventy-seven. In true Egyptian style he had prepared for his own death twenty-four years earlier when he had built himself a mausoleum – a pyramid based on the design of the Tomb of Cestius in Rome. Legend had it that 'Mad Jack' was buried sitting up in full evening dress, wearing his top hat, at an iron table laid for dinner with a bottle of port at arm's length. The floor was said to be strewn with broken glass against the day the Devil came to 'claim his own'. Unfortunately when in 1938 the rotten wooden door was removed for repair it was found that 'Mad Jack' had in fact been buried the conventional way beneath the floor of the tomb.

FARLEY MONUMENT, *Nr Winchester, Hampshire*

To commemorate his beloved horse Chalk Pit local squire Paulet St John had built over its grave a thirty-foot tall pyramid, high on Farley Down, a few miles southeast of Winchester. A plaque on the monument reads:

> Underneath lies buried a horse, the property of Paulet St John Esq, that in the month of September 1733 leaped into a chalk pit twenty five feet deep Foxhunting with his master on his back. And in October 1734 he won the Hunters Plate on Worthy Downs and was rode by his owner and entered in the name Chalk Pit.

In September the fox hunting season would not have commenced and Paulet St John would have been out cubbing. For his horse suddenly to arrive at, and then jump, a twenty-five-foot pit must have been quite a feat. St John was a cousin of another pyramid-builder, Francis Douce (1677–1760), who was buried in the pyramid that he had had built for himself in the churchyard of Saint Andrews at Nether Wallop. Both men were related to the more famous pyramid-builder, 'Mad Jack' Fuller of Brightling, East Sussex.

WALES

PENTRE IFAN BURIAL CHAMBER,

Nr Nevern, Dyfed

Pentre Ifan is one of Wales's most impressive megalithic monuments. This cromlech was originally used as a communal burial chamber. Its enormous sixteen-foot-long capstone sits precariously on just three tall, upright stones. Excavations during the 1930s and 1950s show that the burial chamber originally lay within a large oval pit, and that the mound of earth covering it was up to 130 feet long. Once known as Arthur's Quoit, Pentre Ifan in fact means Ivan's Village. Overlooking Pembrokeshire's National Park and, in the distance, Cardigan Bay, Pentre Ifan is to the east of Mynydd Carningli's summit, which is where Saint Brynach is said to have been looked after by angels.

Miss Bridget Golightly stood at the door. 'No, Father Bernard Lordan is busy, but you can come in and buy a book of raffle tickets', she said. I had come to look at a piece of wood reputed to have come from the cask that had carried the relics of St Winefride to Shrewsbury Abbey in 1138. Much reduced in size since a former church warden had spent years cutting splinters off to sell to pilgrims for a shilling a time, it was now not much bigger than the palm of Miss Golightly's hand, and was kept in the church safe.

She told me that she had been inspired by the legend of St Winefride and had been 'in service' at St Winefride's for sixty-two years. For most of those years she had said her prayers walking down the steps into the well's ice-cold mountain water until it reached her neck. Slowly bending her knees, she would immerse herself fully, get out and then repeat the immersion twice more before finally bathing in the plunge pool where she had, on occasion, as tradition bade, knelt on the St Beuno Stone and finished saying her prayers. Miss Golightly had performed this penance at six o'clock in the morning for most of her life.

According to tradition, Winefride was the beautiful daughter of a local prince called Tewyth and his wife Gwenlo, who lived in the seventh century. St Beuno was her uncle, a Celtic holy man. One day Caradoc, a chieftain from Hawardew, returned from a hunting trip and in a drunken state tried to seduce Winefride. She retreated to her bedroom, saying she was going to change her dress but in fact escaped from an open window and ran towards her uncle's baptistry for safety. Caradoc was furious and gave chase. They reached the chapel together and, while remonstrating with her, he drew his sword and sliced off her head. It fell to the ground. St Beuno, on hearing the commotion, came out of his baptistry, quickly picked Winefride's head up and replaced it on her torso. He prayed and raised her to life. Where her head had fallen, a spring of water gushed forth and this is now the Holy Well. St Beuno cursed Caradoc and his family. Caradoc disappeared into the ground and his family barked like dogs for the rest of their lives. Winefride became a nun and bore a white scar which encircled her neck. After her uncle left the area she departed for Gwytherin where she was eventually to become the Abbess.

In Wales there are over one thousand holy wells. St Winefride's Well is one of the very few that still has a pilgrimage tradition. Most of the others are now in ruin. For thousands of years water has been venerated as a life-giving force and has been seen, because of this, to have magical and mysterious powers of healing. Over the centuries many thousands of pilgrims have travelled great distances to take the water and pray for a cure. Everything from rickets, cancer and eye sores to stomach disorders, headaches and infertility can be cured at the appropriate holy well. Though pagan in origin, over the centuries these wells have been Christianized. Saints' names have been attached to them; after all, the first Celtic holy men baptized early Christian Celts in their waters. As their small churches grew, larger parish churches were built, often using some of the stones from the first baptistries. In Wales there are over three hundred churches built over or very near to wells. The practice of leaving an offering 'in thanks', after having taken the waters, was common. This could be a bent pin to exorcise the devil, a piece of rag to transfer the illness to, or most commonly, an offering of money. The church was soon to take advantage of this practice and collecting boxes were left for pilgrims' offerings. These could be quite considerable. In 1413, at Our Lady's Well in Whitekirk, Scotland, over 1500 people visited the well and about £1000 was collected by the monks.

In the cold, damp morning air, when the dawn is slowly lifting and low banks of cloud part, Pentre Ifan, near Nevern, is bathed in a golden light. The mist that envelops it vanishes and the hills around and the valley below become crystal clear. There is silence but for the coo of early morning doves, and the majestic monument can be seen at its loveliest. Three huge upright stones dramatically hold an enormous capstone securely in place. The structure was once covered by an extensive earth mound, with timber and dry stone walls to retain the soil, though all this has now been eroded away. These burial

BRYN CELLI DDU, *Nr Llanddaniel Fab, Anglesey*

Bryn Celli Ddu, or 'hill in a dark grove', started as a henge or ritual enclosure surrounded by a bank and entrance ditch. At a later date a passage burial chamber was added. During excavations in the nineteenth and twentieth centuries two flint arrow heads were found, along with limpet and mussel shells, a stone bead and a burnt human ear bone. This beautifully shaped mound is what now remains of a Neolithic passage grave. The grave is entered from the north-east. The passage is twenty-seven feet long and three feet wide, and brings you out into an eight-foot-wide chamber covered by two capstones. To the west there is a carefully shaped four-foot-tall, cylindrical, free-standing pillar; in the south wall a spiral-carved stone slab, which must have had some mystical significance. Tacitus mentions in a dispatch to Rome in AD 61 that there were still Druid elders in Anglesey.

places are called long barrows because they are longer than they are wide. They are the earliest of the burial tombs that Neolithic man built, and vary in length from about eighty feet to over two hundred feet. To the Neolithic farmers who built them, these huge and awesome buildings must surely have been the focal point of their simple lives. Before being buried, a community's dead were placed in a mortuary house and there they stayed until some significant occasion arose. Then the disarticulated bones, as well as the fresher cadavers, were placed in the long barrows. Grave goods did not usually accompany these burials though, on occasion, stone axes, scrapers and fragments of burnt and broken pottery have been found amongst the bones. Once a long barrow had been sealed – and it could contain anything from a handful of bodies to over fifty – it was rarely opened again.

Neolithic people also built what we now call passage graves. Like long barrows, they too were covered with massive earth mounds. Passage graves are characterized by a single chamber in the centre of the mound, entered by a long low creep passage. Bryn Celli Ddu in Anglesey is probably the best example in Wales of this type of monument. Here in the tall central chamber a human ear bone was found in a shallow pit dug in the centre of the floor. In a corner, one slab is carved with a spiral and standing in another corner there is a mysterious, smooth, free-standing cylindrical pillar, which undoubtedly played some part in early man's ritual observances. A stone bench was also created where some of the dead were probably laid out. The remains of a sacrificial ox were found in a grave outside the entrance.

Chamber tombs were a further and last Neolithic refinement, once again looking similar on the outside to long barrows and passage graves. But inside these tombs the area was divided up into various chambers. Unlike the earlier long barrows these tombs were used for periods of up to a thousand years. Inhumation was practised, the deceased being buried in a sitting, lying or squatting position. During excavations it has been discovered that large bones as well as skulls often seem to have been removed. These were probably taken for use in ritual ceremonies. Grave goods were part of these burials as they were deemed to assist the deceased soul in its afterlife.

MAEN LLIA,
Nr Ystradfellte, Powys

Maen Llia is a few hundred yards off the minor road leading from Ystradfellte to Heol Senni in the Brecon Beacon National Park. This huge standing stone is diamond shaped, and one feels that this alone must have some significance we are yet to understand. It looks magnificent in the Llia Valley, standing twelve feet tall and nine feet wide, but only two feet thick. Legend has it that whenever the cocks crow the stone moves off to drink in the nearby River Nedd.

ARTHUR'S STONE, *Reynoldston, West Glamorgan*

Arthur's Stone holds a commanding position on Cefyn Bryn Common overlooking Loughor estuary and Llanelli to the north, a mile from the village of Reynoldston on the Gower Peninsula. The two huge stones are the remains of what was once a Neolithic burial chamber. The larger wedge-shaped stone is known as Arthur's Stone and is estimated to weigh over twenty-five tons. According to legend, the stone was removed by King Arthur from his boot while travelling to the battle of Camlann in AD 539. He threw the stone over his shoulder, it landed on the common and has remained there ever since. At one time local girls who had doubts about their lovers' fidelity could 'test them at the stones', by placing honey-cakes soaked in milk on the smaller of the two stones at midnight during a full moon. They then had to crawl on their hands and knees three times around the stones. If their lovers were faithful, it is said they would then join them.

CAPEL GARMON CHAMBERED TOMB, *Nr Rhydlanfair, Gwynedd*

This magnificent Neolithic chambered tomb with a false entrance is situated in a dramatic setting looking westward towards the Cambrian mountains of north Wales. It can be reached from a minor road leading north from Rhydlanfair on the A5, a few miles south-east of Betws-y-coed. Sited in a field, but well-signposted, a little way from Tyn-y-coed farm, this now restored and excavated tomb has in the past been known as The Cave. It is open to the sky except for the western chamber, which is still covered by a fourteen-foot capstone, probably because up until the last century it was used as a stable for farm animals, which entered it along the opened 'false' entrance, the original Neolithic entrance being to the south of the tomb.

ST LYTHANS AND TINKINSWOOD BURIAL CHAMBERS, *St Nicholas, South Glamorgan*

Two megalithic burial chambers lie a short distance from each other near the village of St Nicholas. Both are in good condition and date from about 4000 BC. At Tinkinswood, also known as the Long Cairn, the huge capstone is over twenty-four feet long and weighs over forty tons. It is believed to be the largest in Britain. The site was excavated in 1914 and the remains of over fifty bodies, along with pottery, were found. Nearby the smaller chamber known as St Lythans stands alone on a mound in a farmer's field. Its capstone sits squarely upon three upright stones, and now acts as a shelter for sheep that graze the land. Both burial chambers have interesting myths attached to them. You can chance your luck by sleeping out overnight at Tinkinswood on the eve of May Day, St Johns Day (June 23rd) or Midwinter's Day. The Druids are said to have put a curse on the stones and you will either go mad, die or become a poet. The wedge-shaped capstone at St Lythans is said to spin around three times each Midsummer's Eve. The field is said to be barren, cursed once again by the Druids, and all wishes made standing in front of the chamber on Hallowe'en will come true.

the hillside. The dog refused and sheltered in the stone kennel. The giant was furious, took up his staff and hurled it at the kennel, but it missed. The staff – a tall, slim, pointed monolith – can be seen stuck in the ground about one hundred yards away.

THE DRUIDS CIRCLE, *Nr Conwy, Gwynedd*

The Druids Circle is at the junction of several ancient pathways on an exposed plateau with striking views across Conwy Bay. A minor road leads up from Penmaenmaw. The Druids Circle now comprises over twenty stones, some of which are clearly shaped, though many have fallen. It is about ninety feet in diameter. During excavations three cists were found in the centre containing cremated children, along with a Bronze Age knife and food vessels. It is thought that these children were sacrificial offerings rather than ordinary burials. Two of the stones have legends attached to them. One is called the Deity Stone and is reputed to bend over and hit anyone using bad language near it. The stone opposite has a bowl carved into the top surface. Young babies can be brought luck and good health if placed in it soon after birth. Witches' sabbaths are reputed to have taken place here, and at the climax of one, the stones spoke out, so terrifying two witches that they instantly died. A third went mad.

THE POET'S STONE, *Nr Roewen, Gwynedd*

This Neolithic long barrow stands beside a Roman road leading up from the village of Roewen. Resting on four uprights the rectangular capstone is two and a half feet thick, eight feet wide and thirteen feet long. A little of the original mound still survives. The stone is also known as the Greyhound's Kennel after a legend that tells of a local giant who lived on nearby Tal y Fan. One day he sent his dog out in foul weather to bring the sheep in from

PENRHOS FEILW STANDING STONES, *Nr Holyhead, Anglesey*

There are at least thirty-nine megalithic stones in Anglesey. The Penrhos Feilw standing stones are perhaps the most beautiful and unusual. They are just ten feet apart, and eleven feet tall, in the centre of a field to the east of the Holyhead mountains. They are probably Bronze Age and, according to a long but unsubstantiated tradition, they were at the centre of a stone circle, now unfortunately destroyed. Between them a cist was found that contained bones, as well as a spear and arrow heads. These two enigmatic stones line up with the 'Ghost' stone and with the Holyhead Mountain Hut Circles, which some now believe to be of Bronze Age origin.

THE FOUR STONES, *Nr Old Radnor, Powys*

This Bronze Age ceremonial site is simply called The Four Stones. It is situated in a field near a minor road leading from Old Radnor to Kinnerton. All four stones are positioned very close together, and three are much larger than the other. All seem to have been artificially rounded. It is said that they mark the place where four Welsh princes fell in battle and, each Midsummer's Night, they are mysteriously covered in blood. The story goes that a wicked witch turned the four princes into stone; she herself is now entombed in stone in Hindwell Pool, where the stones quench their thirst while listening to the church clock strike midnight.

HAROLD'S STONES, *Trelleck, Gwent*

Trelleck was once a major medieval settlement – one of the largest in
Wales. It takes its name from three tall standing stones in a field at the edge
of the village. The spelling is a corruption of the words *tre* or *tri* meaning
three, and *lech* meaning stone. The stones are thought to have been erected
by Bronze Age man. Some say they are the remains of a stone circle, and
others that they were used for astrological alignments. According to legend
they are called Harold's Stones because they commemorate a great battle
King Harold won over the Britons. Another story tells how the
Herefordshire giant, Jack O' Kent, threw them down from Ysgyryd Fawr
while playing Pitch and Toss with the Devil.

The beautiful sundial in Trelleck Church depicts the stones, and is dated
1689, while the local inn, called The Lion, has a pub sign showing the
stones set in an African plain along with a shaggy-maned lion.

THE GREAT CROSS, ST BRYNACH CHURCH, *Nevern, Dyfed*

Walk up the dark and sombre avenue of six-hundred-year-old Irish yew trees at Nevern. One of them is known as the Bleeding Yew, because of the blood-like sap that has flowed from a bough ever since an innocent man was hung from it for sheep stealing. You will come to Wales's most famous Celtic cross. Standing thirteen feet tall and carved in the tenth or eleventh century it holds mysteries that will probably never be fathomed. On all four sides there are carved panels that hold intricate and endlessly interlacing ribbon designs – possibly symbols of eternity. Two panels on the east face depict a primitive form of cross with angular arms indicating rotation against the sun. On the east and west faces are abbreviated inscriptions in a peculiar alphabet found in the earliest British writing. These words have never been fully deciphered. On Patrons Day, April 7th, the first cuckoo of spring is said to sing from the top of the Great Cross. On one occasion the bird was late and, scarcely able to sound a note, fell dead.

FIVE FACED FONT, ST GWRTHWL'S CHURCH, *Llanwrthwl, Powys*

Just to the right of the south-facing porch is a large monolith known as the 'preachers stone'. St Gwrthwl is said to have addressed his first congregation from this site and probably founded his church here because the site was already venerated. Inside this beautifully restored church is an ancient font, said to be twelfth-century or earlier. It was brought here after the Dissolution and possibly came from the Cistercian monastery at Abbey Cwmhir. It is one of several 'five faced' fonts found in the area.

ST WINEFRIDE'S WELL, *Holywell, Clwyd*

St Winefride's Well and chapel are on the edge of the small Welsh town that takes its name, Holywell. This is the Lourdes of Britain, and every year thousands of pilgrims flock here to take the water and pray for a cure. During the Well season a service is held each morning and on Dedication Day, which is now the first Sunday following June 22nd, services and immersions take place throughout the daylight hours. St Winefride's Well is the oldest well in Britain with a continuous pilgrimage tradition. Catholics have been praying here and performing total immersion penances in these waters for over 1300 years. Tradition states that where Winefride's head fell, after being sliced off by Caradoc in the seventh-century, a spring gushed forth. This is now the Holy Well. Her life was saved by her uncle St Beuno, a seventh century Celtic holy man, who placed her head back on her torso, prayed and brought her back to life.

THE ROMAN STEPS, *Nr Llanbedr, Gwynedd*

Old trade routes in Wales run west to east, connecting the poor mountain settlements with the more prosperous lowland England. One such remote, and possibly misnamed, route is the Roman Steps. Follow the mountain, and often single-lane road east out of the coastal town of Llanbedr, a few miles south of Harlech. Winding and climbing through an ancient tree-covered hillside, you eventually emerge at a lonely, clear and beautiful mountain lake called Llyn Cwn Bychan. Follow a track upwards through a wood and start the climb up the heather- and boulder-covered Rhinogs mountains. As you near the summit the track turns into a fine and well-worn pathway – the Roman Steps. The scene – wild goats and an incredible view – can be no different now than it was a thousand years ago for the traders who used this route to transport gold from the mine at Bony Dbu.

THE PILLAR OF ELISEG, *Nr Llangollen, Clwyd*

The Pillar of Eliseg inspired the name Valle Crucis – Valley of the Cross – for this splendid spot a few miles north of Llangollen, en route to the Horse Shoe Pass, next to the ruined Valle Crucis Abbey. A thirty-one line inscription in Insular script (a writing developed by sixth-century monasteries), now too badly weathered to be legible, records, according to a translation made by the scholar Edward Llwyd in 1696, that the cross was erected by Cyngen, Prince of Powys for his warlike great-grandfather Eliseg. Cromwell's soldiers tore the cross down during the Civil War and for many years it lay broken. When it was re-erected the mound on which it stood was opened. A skeleton was found inside, buried in a blue stone cist, along with a large silver coin. Mysteriously no coinage was in circulation at the time of the burial. The skull was removed and gilded before being re-buried with the bones.

SCOTLAND

Scotland possesses some of Britain's most enigmatic and spectacular megalithic monuments. Many, due to their remoteness, are hardly ever visited but the journey is an experience and the visit often awe-inspiring.

Leaving Ullapool, the west coast fishing port at the mouth of Loch Broom, where the lowering dark skies meet the inky olive green seas, short-lived gilded pools of light illuminate a succession of craggy islands – Martin, Bottle, Summer, Horse and Priest. Past the factory fishing vessels, it is a three-hour journey across open sea to the principal town of the Western Isles – Stornoway. Callanish, which is no more than a straggle of crofts, is less than an hour's drive away from Stornoway, over rolling, heather-covered countryside. The magnificent megalithic Stones stand for all to see on a rise overlooking Loch Roag, and nearby there are three smaller stone circles stretching out across the glittering, loch-riddled landscape.

Many believe the Callanish Standing Stones to be second only in importance to Stonehenge. Hardly known and in comparison rarely visited, this Neolithic monument is set out in a shape similar to that of a Celtic cross. At its centre is a massive fifteen-foot slab. To the north an avenue of stones runs for 250 yards, while shorter arms stretch out to the south, west and east.

According to Professor Alexander Thom, an eminent Oxford mathematician who, along with his son Archie, spent a lifetime plotting and calculating Neolithic alignments, Neolithic man set up these stones to mark the movement of the moon from one solstice to another. But amazingly he believed, as others still do, that this huge Neolithic 'computer' was also designed to calculate to a precise degree the passage of time, and also the points to which the moon would travel during its 18.61-year cycle. At the furthest points of the structure the sun, the moon and the earth are aligned. This

RING OF BRODGAR,
Nr Stromness, Orkney

This huge and spectacular stone circle is built on an isthmus overlooking the lochs of Stenness to the west and Harray to the east, just off the main road between the towns of Stromness and Kirkwall in the Orkneys. Carefully laid out in measurements of 2.72 feet, or one megalithic yard, this perfect circle is 340 feet or 125 megalithic yards in diameter. Twenty-seven of the original sixty stones remain. The tallest stone is fifteen feet high. All are made of local red sandstone, which splits easily and naturally. In the eighteenth century, the Ring was known as 'The Temple of the Sun', and was the site of feasting and dancing on New Year's Day.

phenomenon was not noted until Sir Isaac Newton rediscovered it as late as the seventeenth century, and it is known to modern astronomers as the 'eclipse season'.

Thousands of years ago the sleepy valley of Kilmartin on the west coast of Scotland was alive with the activity of Neolithic and later Bronze Age man. These early farmers, fishermen and traders have left us an array of unique and unusual megalithic monuments. Kilmartin is famous for its linear cairn cemetery stretching out over three miles. Nether Largie South, a Neolithic tomb, was the first structure to be built, and the others were to follow over the next 2000 years. A beautiful jadite axe head was found in one, so delicate it could only have had some ritual significance; petrological examination shows that it came from the Alps. A jet bead was found in another tomb, and in yet another the famous Poltalloch Bronze Age necklace, perhaps one of the most beautiful ever discovered, comprising over one hundred barrel-shaped beads; the remains of human skeletons and the burnt bones of an ox were also found in a tomb on the site, while an axe head design (considered to be the symbol of a great warrior) picked out on a stone slab making up part of the cist can be seen in Ri Cruin cairn.

Nearby is the romantically named Templewood Stone Circle thought to have been the haunt of Druids. On one of the stones is a spiral carving, now unfortunately very faint, but similar to others found in the area. It is possible that 'cup' and 'ring' marks and spiral carvings were symbols for Bronze Age gods.

Along the valley there are several alignments of standing stones. One of the most interesting is the Ballymeanoch 'cup'-marked stone. Two rows of huge blocks stand face to face 150 yards apart. The most easterly are the largest – four enormous, twelve-foot slabs graduated in height. The tallest are to the south. The second slab's easterly face is covered with a mass of well-defined 'cup' marks. Nearby is the now-fallen perforated stone used in the last century to seal marriage vows. Further along the valley are other aligned stones, testament to the importance of this valley to prehistoric man.

The Orkneys, like their westerly sister islands, are a megalithic dream. Maes Howe, the Ring of Brodgar, the Stones of Stenness, the Dwarfie Stane and the more recent Pictish stone in St Mary's church on South Ronaldsay, are just a few of the sites that

RUNES, MAES HOWE, *Nr Stromness, Orkney*
Runes are one of the earliest forms of alphabet and were used by Scandinavians and Germanic peoples. They are said to possess magic qualities, and were often used to ward off evil spirits and witches. Odin, chief of the gods, is said to have invented them, styling himself Lord of the Runes. The above script is inscribed in the Maes Howe burial tomb on the Orkney Islands (see page 138).

can be visited on these flat, windblown, North Sea islands, just across the Pentland Firth from John O'Groats.

The Tomb of the Eagle is dramatically set near the cliff's edge overlooking the North Sea on the island of South Ronaldsay. The tomb was discovered untouched on farmland and the farmer, Ronald Simison, excavated it over many years with the help of a team of archaeologists. Their finds were extraordinary and have thrown new light on the life of Neolithic man. The building of the tomb took over 1000 years and in that time only three hundred and forty-two people were buried there. Not a single whole skeleton was found but over 16,000 disarticulated bones. It is thought that the dead were probably left out in the open on mortuary slabs. The elements and birds would, after a period of time, leave only the heavier bones. Then on an auspicious occasion the bones and the skull would be interned, the skulls placed together with the carcasses of white-tailed sea eagles, thought to be totems of these people.

Nearby is the tiny, isolated church of St Mary's, Burwick. Sitting alone on the bay's edge, with no electricity and only a gas lamp and chandelier for illumination, this is the home of the largely unexplained four-foot-long, rounded Grey Whinstone, which has a pair of shod feet cut into it. I was told it had no name by the crofter that held the key to the church, and who had lived near the church all his eighty years. He was surprised I was interested in the stone. 'Only a few people a year come and look at it,' he said. When questioned as to its origin and purpose, he remembered that 'you'd stand on it to confess to your maker' – an interesting thought and perhaps true. But the incised stone is much older than Christianity. It was probably a Pictish inauguration stone. A clan chief or king would, before assuming office, literally step into his predecessor's shoes, thus symbolically marking the line of succession. A much fainter but similar stone can be found in Clickhimin in the Shetlands, and there is another at Dunadd.

At Hoy, the now sparsely populated and most southerly Orcadian island, made famous by the Old Man of Hoy, can be found the unique Dwarfie Stane; the home, according to legend, of a troll and his wife, who managed to cut into solid rock and carve out two sleeping chambers. One even contains a rock-cut pillow. In the bar of the

BALLYMEANOCH STANDING STONES, *Nr Kilmartin, Argyllshire, Strathclyde*
Just off the Dunadd to Kilmartin road, lying in a cultivated field, are two unusual parallel stone rows. They are aligned north-south. The larger of the rows now contains four huge slabs. One of these has been heavily 'cup' marked, and these are still clearly visible. The smaller row lying about 150 feet away now comprises of only two slabs. Nearby is a very ruinous henge monument, with two cists, and an outlyer that has now fallen but was, until the last century, used in ceremonies to seal marriage vows.

only hostelry, I was told of how a fire had swept through the hillside a few years previously. Burning back the heather, it exposed an array of Neolithic and Bronze Age tombs. A young archaeologist from the mainland had spent several months over the winter carrying out exploratory excavations, with the aim of raising money for a much fuller and more detailed dig. His efforts were to no avail, he was unable to raise any money and these unexplored tombs are now being left to future generations to rediscover and marvel over. But what was really surprising was that my informant, while suggesting that the tombs would bring tourists and their much-needed money to the island, went on to say that it didn't matter anyhow if these prehistoric tombs were ploughed up and lost. Others would be found; the island had too many!

Maes Howe on mainland Orkney is a remarkable Neolithic passage tomb built in 2700 BC. This large grave is probably one of the wonders of the prehistoric world, and certainly the finest example of a Neolithic tomb in Britain. It is entered via a low, narrow, south-west-facing 'creep' passage. When in place, the blocking stone would have left a chink which only allowed the last light from a midwinter sunset to penetrate the tomb and strike at the base of the central burial chamber. Built with extreme precision and using no mortar, every block is still solid 4500 years after being put in place. Maes Howe also contains a large collection of Runic writing left by Norsemen who broke into the tomb in the twelfth century in search of treasure. Some of the writing has been translated: 'A great treasure is hidden in the north west', 'Happy is he who might find the great treasure', 'These Runes were carved by the man most skilled in Runes in the Western Ocean'. In fact the treasure these Viking graffiti artists were after was probably not Neolithic. There is evidence of the rebuilding of the outer bank in the ninth century, perhaps by an early Viking chief who settled on the island and was eventually buried there with his wealth.

DUNADD STONE FOOTPRINT,
Nr Lochgilphead, Argyllshire, Strathclyde

A few miles north of Lochgilphead on the road to Kilmartin, entirely alone and standing out from the waterlogged fields that must once have been a wet wasteland, but easily missed in this dramatic Scottish landscape, is the fortified rock of Dunadd. This was the centre of the Scottish kingdom of Dalriada founded by Fergus Mor in AD 500, believed to have been in use for over two centuries. Near the summit is a large, flat bedrock into which has been cut a footprint; a bowl has also been carved into the rock. These are both thought to have been used in the ritual inauguration of the kings and chieftains of Dalriada, the footprint denoting the act of symbolically stepping into a predecessor's shoes.

While I was there, two women stepped into the print 'for luck' and confirmed it to be a size six.

THE CALLANISH STANDING STONES, *Callanish, Isle of Lewis, Outer Hebrides*

This remarkable and truly enigmatic megalithic monument stands on a hill overlooking Loch Roag on the west coast of the Outer Hebridean island of Lewis. Considered by many to be second only in importance to Stonehenge, but in comparison hardly visited, this site has been seen to have been astrologically aligned with various large stars, the sun and the moon, and with distinctive points on the horizon. Though it can be seen from miles around, this flattened circle is only twenty-two feet across. Thirteen tall 'undressed' stones made from the easily-split local gneiss surround a very small, nearly equally divided, stone burial tomb. There is a nearly parallel avenue of nineteen stones leading up to the circle and beyond, and two other arms leading to the west and east. From above, the complex resembles a Celtic cross.

The stones have acquired many legends; one associated with famine tells of a white sea cow who befriended a woman wading into the sea to commit suicide. She was told to go with her friends each night to the circle where the cow would fill a pail of milk for each of them. One night a witch appeared and milked the cow into a sieve, and it subsequently disappeared. Another story claims that any marriage consummated within the circle will be a particularly happy one. A third claims that the stones represent thirteen giants who refused to become Christians. Angered, St Kieran turned them to stone.

THE LONG GREY HORNED CAIRN OF CAMSTER, *Nr Lybster, Caithness, Highland*

In a heathery, boggy moorland setting a few miles north of Lybster on a minor road leading to the village of Watten lies the enormous and unusually shaped Long Grey Horned Cairn of Camster. This Neolithic burial tomb encompasses two beehive burial chambers, built at different times. The most northerly burial chamber at the head of the long cairn was probably built first. It has a round retaining wall, which its partner does not. Human and animal bones as well as flints were found in both burial chambers. Why the cairns at a later date were covered with several thousand tons of stone, elongated, and given a most unusual profile, we will never know. It will also remain a mystery why a raised platform was built between the 'horns' at the head of the cairn. The Grey Horned Cairn is only 600 feet away from the Grey Camster Round Cairn, and all three burial chambers can be entered by crawling through very long, low and narrow passages.

CAIRNHOLY II, *Nr Creetown, Kirkcudbrightshire, Dumfries and Galloway*

Cairnholy I and II are off the A75 between Gatehouse of Fleet and Creetown, up a farmtrack, but clearly marked from the road. Cairnholy II is on higher ground overlooking Wigtown Bay, about 150 yards north of Cairnholy I. This spectacular Neolithic tomb, with a nine-foot portal stone, was blocked after final use 3000 years ago. During excavations in 1949 flints, pottery and a scraper from the Neolithic period were found. Cairnholy is a derivative of Carn Ulaidh meaning 'treasured cairn'. Cairns such as these were often thought to hold great wealth but local people were usually too afraid to open them for fear of vengeance from their gods.

MAES HOWE, *Nr Stromness, Orkney*

Undoubtedly one of the wonders of the prehistoric world, this Neolithic burial tomb was built in 2700 BC. The grass-covered mound is over one hundred feet in diameter and twenty-five feet tall. It is made of alternate layers of stone clay and peat, concealing a burial tomb that is entered along a 'creep' passage. The tomb contains three chambers built into the walls and is fifteen feet square and twelve feet tall. Each chamber was sealed by a blocking stone, now lying on the floor. Maes Howe was broken into during the twelfth century by Vikings, who left a series of twenty-four Runic inscriptions. Translated, some of these read: 'A long time ago a great treasure (was) hidden here', 'Ingibiorg the fair widow' and 'Hakon single handed bore treasure from this howe'.

THE TOMB OF THE EAGLE, *Nr Lidder, Orkney*

The Tomb of the Eagle, an early Neolithic chamber tomb, is dramatically set near the cliff's edge overlooking the North Sea on the island of South Ronaldsay in the Orkneys. Because of its completeness the tomb can be shown to have been under construction for over 200 years; but even more astonishing, it can be seen to have been in use and to have been the centre of a tribal subgroup's ritual ceremonies for a period in excess of 1000 years. Animals were sacrificed and their meat left, beef on the outside, lamb on the inside. A pile of shallow-water fish was left at the entrance to the tomb. The tomb yielded a polished jade button, a broken necklace, hammers and scrapers, and a beautifully-made stone mace head. A large pile of broken and decorated pottery from at least forty-three different vessels was found to have been burnt before being entombed. 16,000 disarticulated human bones were discovered, coming from 342 people, but there was not a single complete skeleton in the tomb. Amongst the bones were the carcasses of magnificent white-tailed sea eagles – perhaps totems of these people.

THE STONES OF STENNESS, *Nr Stromness, Orkney*

The Stones of Stenness are older than their partner, the Ring of Brodgar, to which they were probably connected by an avenue of stones, as at Avebury. The monument has been dated at 3000 BC and is now much depleted; only three of the original twelve stones are still standing. Two other smaller stones have recently been added. The ditch and bank that encircled the stones has now all but disappeared, having been ploughed out over many years. Nevertheless it is still a very impressive monument, the tallest stone being over sixteen feet high. The eighteenth-century antiquarian Dr Robert Henry noted that local people celebrated at the stones after church on New Year's Day. If a man and a woman fell in love they would go first to 'The Temple of the Moon', 'where the woman, in the presence of the man, fell down on her knees and prayed to the god Wodden that he would enable her to perform all promises and obligations she had made to the young man'. The couple then went to the 'Temple of the Sun' (at the Ring of Brodgar),

'where the man prayed in a similar manner before the woman'. They then went to the Holed Stone of Odin (now destroyed) and clasped hands through it and made an oath of fidelity.

THE DWARFIE STANE, *Whaness, Orkney*

'Hoy' means high, and 'the High Island' is the largest in the Orkneys, after Mainland. It lies between Mainland and Scotland, separated only by the Pentland Firth. The Dwarfie Stane is a third of a mile over boggy, heather-covered moorland between the hamlets of Whaness and Rackwick and the Old Man of Hoy. In a large, glaciated, open valley between Ward Hill and the Dwarfie Hammers this unique Neolithic rock-cut tomb was chiselled out of solid red sandstone. A short entry passage leads in and, on either side, separated by a two-inch lip, are two 'cells', each about four feet long, three feet wide and two and a half feet high. The 'cell' on the right has a pillow of uncut rock at its inner end. A blocking stone slides in to seal the tomb, another that was cut for use lies a little way behind. There are no other rocks in the valley of comparable size, and tradition has it that a giant in Caithness, angered with the island people, hurled the rock across the Pentland Firth. His strength was great, but not great enough to get the rock over Ward Hill, and it fell where it now lies. It was later found by a local troll who made it into a home for himself and his wife.

EAST AQUHORTHIES STONE CIRCLE, *Nr Inverurie,*
Aberdeenshire, Grampian

East Aquhorthies recumbent stone circle is nearly three miles west of Inverurie off a dead-end road, running past East Aquhorthies farm. This well-cared-for Bronze Age monument is signposted and easy to find. Lying within the shadow of Ben Achie, and built on sloping ground, this circle with a diameter of sixty-three feet comprises of nine uprights and a huge recumbent stone, which is made of a different material from the other stones. As always there are two tall, shaped, flanking stones. They are all linked together by an enclosing bank. Some authorities see this grouping as symbolic of the ritual blocking of a chamber tomb, with the smaller low-lying stones on either side marking the entrance way. Others consider that the recumbent stone and two flankers act as a 'windowframe' for observing the moon in the southern sky. As with other stone circles there is a diamond-shaped stone and a 'waisted', rectangular stone, similar to those found at The Hurlers and Avebury. There are also triangular-shaped stones similar to those found at the Scorhill Stone Circle.

TEMPLEWOOD STONE CIRCLE AND CIST,
Nr Kilmartin, Argyllshire, Strathclyde

This Bronze Age stone circle was used for ceremonial purposes between 1500 and 2000 BC. It is now centred on a small slab cist, which once contained the body of a child, a beaker and some flints. Today this is surrounded by only thirteen of the original forty stones. The northernmost stone has, near its base, a spiral inscribed on to it, which is now very faint.

Templewood Stone Circle is adjacent to another smaller circle and also the great, linear, Bronze Age Nether Largie Barrows, as well as other stone monuments. Given to the Scottish nation in 1932 by Sir Ian Malcolm of Poltalloch, it got its name during the Romantic movement of the eighteenth century. A grove of oak trees was planted here. This and other Bronze Age monuments in the valley were preserved as they were seen to enhance the landscape.

HILL O' MANY STANES, *Nr Lybster, Caithness, Highland*

The Hill O' Many Stanes is off the A9, a few miles north of Lybster en route to Wick, John O' Groats, and the summer-only ferry to Burwick, South Ronaldsay in the Orkneys. Bronze Age and built on the slope of a small hill, this unique grouping of over two hundred stones has no well-explained rationale. All the stones are about three feet tall and run in twenty-two, nearly parallel lines; 'nearly parallel' because, with careful plotting, it can be shown that the grid is in fact fan-shaped. This type of monument is unique to Caithness and Sutherland, although a similar grid which uses larger stones can be found in Brittany.

ABERLEMMO SYMBOL STONE, *Aberlemmo, Angus, Tayside*

On a grass verge by the B9134 just outside Aberlemmo are three Pictish incised stones. The earliest and least understood is the so-called Symbol Stone. Over four feet tall, and in recent years moved from the adjacent field to join the other two stones, this natural shaped monolith is deeply incised with a 'serpent', a 'double disc and Z rod', and a 'mirror and comb' symbol. On the reverse and near the base are some prehistoric 'cup' marks. The code to decipher these and many other 'real life' symbols has never been broken, though it has now been suggested that these Pictish symbols were the unique identification marks of a Pict warrior. These stones do not appear to be sepulchral but may be boundary markers. Little is known of the Picts. Pictland was what is now northern Scotland, and many legends have grown up around these 'small, wild, heathen, painted people', who on occasion came south to harry the Romans. They were eventually converted to Christianity, and their Pictish Cross Slabs bear witness to this.

ST MARY'S CHURCH STONE, *Burwick, Orkney*

St Mary's Church, Burwick, is at the southernmost end of South Ronaldsay, connected to the mainland by the A961. Flat, treeless, windy and very wild, Burwick is little more than three crofts, a ruined farm, and the little church of St Mary, sitting on the edge of the bay. The church was built in 1789, near the site of the first chapel in the Orkneys, and nothing much has changed here for a long time. The church is still lit only by a gas lamp and a simple candle chandelier. In the room next to the vestry, lying in one corner, is a curious and largely unexplained four-foot-long stone. This rounded Grey Whinstone has a pair of shod footprints cut into it. Possibly used in some Pictish ritual inauguration, there is a similar print in stone in the Shetlands, and another at Dunadd in Scotland.

MIDMAR RECUMBENT STONE CIRCLE, *Nr Echt, Aberdeenshire, Grampian*

Midmar Church of Christ is a few miles west of the village of Echt on the B9119. It was built in 1787, and can be found up the hill from the old and now destroyed St Nidans chapel, named after the far-travelled sixth-century Celtic saint who built his first baptistry here. Behind this grey and rather severe kirk, and within the graveyard lies a beautiful and nearly complete recumbent Bronze Age stone circle. Built of local Hill of Farr stone, and known as The Druids, this is one of three circles in the immediate area. It surrounds a manicured circular lawn and in this Christian setting is a wonderful pagan celebration. A stone is missing – the one that would be closest to the church – and this was apparently used in the foundations of the Church of Christ. As with other recumbent stone circles, the smallest stone is opposite the huge recumbent stone, and the height of the stones increases around the circle, culminating with the two pointed flankers that stand on either side of what was possibly a Bronze Age altar.

DUN CARLOWAY BROCH, *Doune Carloway, Isle of Lewis,*
Outer Hebrides

Dun Carloway Broch is perhaps one of the best preserved brochs, or
fortified homesteads, and is only a short distance from the Callanish
Standing Stones, on the west coast of the Isle of Lewis, overlooking East
Loch Roag and the Great Bernera. Towering over the isolated hamlet of
Doune Carloway this style of Iron Age structure is regarded as being
uniquely Scottish. Nearly 2000 years ago as many as 500 brochs, all of very
similar design and construction, were built in isolated and remote parts of
coastal Scotland. It has been suggested, because of their uniformity in
design and neatness of construction, that they were all built by teams of
professional masons rather than by local people. What caused this rash of
fortified building, and why they were in use for only a little over 200 years,
remains a mystery. All were 'double-skinned' with an internal staircase built
between the walls, which spiralled up to galleries and eventually the roof.
Entrance was via a very small and low doorway in the outer enclosure wall.
At Dun Carloway legend recalls a great battle between local giants and
invading Finns, who were eventually beaten off. A tenth-century clan
tradition tells of cattle thieves who took refuge within the walls being
smothered by burning peat thrown down from above.

CLOUTIE WELL, *Nr Munlochy, Ross and Cromarty, Highland*

The worship of water is pre-Christian and there are many hundreds of 'holy' wells throughout Britain. Today only a handful are venerated, compared to early Christian and pagan times. With the advent of Christianity, pagan water worship was assimilated into the Christian faith. The pagan 'Lady of the Well' became, for example, 'Our Lady'. Besides being a life-giving force, many wells were said to possess remedial properties. St Boniface's Well, better known as the 'Cloutie Well', is believed to be able to cure all kinds of illness but only if a rag, known as a cloutie, is left as an offering, having first been rubbed on the infected area. According to tradition the cloutie should be red. Today many thousands of clouties and bits of clothing are tied to overhanging branches, and are on lines strung up between the trees by the well. The water is most effective if drunk on May 1st or the following Sunday. The Cloutie Well is on the A832 between Tore and Munlochy.

WELL OF HEADS, *Invergarry, Inverness-shire, Highland*

The Well of Heads is situated on the edge of Loch Oich, on the busy A82 just outside Invergarry, and may represent resumption of the pagan Celtic practice of head and water worship. According to legend, on 25 September 1663 Alexander McDonald, the young chief of Keppoch, and his brother Ranald were brutally murdered by rivals within their clan. Two years after their murder, at a Privy Council meeting in Edinburgh, a letter of 'Fire and Sword' was issued against their murderers. At Inverlair the seven murderers were hunted down, killed and decapitated. Their heads were washed in the Well before being taken as proof of death to Invergarry Castle, and from there they were taken and put on display in Edinburgh.

Acknowledgements

I have over the course of researching *Mysterious Britain* used many books for reference. Some of the books mentioned in the bibliography will give a much fuller and more detailed picture of things prehistoric and medieval.

I am particularly grateful to Dr Pamela King of Queen Mary and Westfield College, University of London, who let me make use of some of her research work on cadaverous tombs. I would also like to thank: Rev. Glyn Ackerley, Peter Clark of Royston Town Council, Denise Ashurst, Sophie and Alex Grant (The Tolvan Holed Stone is on private property and permission to view it should be sought from the Grants), Elsbeth Henderson of Historic Scotland, Miss Bridget Golightly, Rev. Trevor Hudson, Father Bernard Lordan, Noel Newton and Mr and Mrs Ronald Simison.

My film was processed with great speed and efficiency by Kodak Professional Processing, Wimbledon.

Photographer's Notes

All these photographs were taken on Nikon cameras. I used Kodachrome 64 and 25 throughout this project. It's a superb film with excellent colour saturation. Cokin graduated filters were used where necessary, not to change but to enhance the picture. Every shot was made with the use of a tripod.

Photographing prehistoric remains, and in particular standing stones, does pose some problems. One large lump of rock can look awfully like another. When I told a friend what I was doing he disparagingly said, 'You mean you're photographing bumps on the landscape!' Well those 'bumps', and especially standing stones, are for the most part incredibly beautiful. Many of them do seem to have a magnetic force that draws you in, and some seem to have character. It's no wonder that in Cornwall they are regarded as 'people'. I have endeavoured to show, and I hope succeeded in showing them at their best, to make them come alive. But of course all this is about patience and light, and I have enjoyed this aspect enormously. Many, many hours have been spent on some desolate hillside watching the clouds and waiting for those elusive rays of afternoon light. There have been many frustrations and wasted journeys, much racing to 'catch' the light before the rain swept in. Too many pre-dawn calls, those tired dark mornings, with only a hope and a prayer that the dawn sunlight would be magical. Unfortunately, too often, I would find a thick grey lining of cloud that masked any hope of success.

Many of the sites I photographed have been in some quiet British backwater, or on a wild windswept moor where time seems to stand still. To be there has truly been an experience. I have travelled through some wonderful countryside. The west coast of Scotland is stunning, in particular the journey going north from Ullapool to Durness and Cape Wrath. Mt Suilven and Canis are spectacular and I was fortunate to be there one afternoon when I watched the mist and rain blow away, turning into a golden evening and bathing the rounded summit and heather-covered lower slopes of Mt Suilven in a mesmeric array of autumnal colours. Though I photographed no people for *Mysterious Britain*, in the course of working on this project I met many, and I have used what some said to me while passing the time of day. I would like to thank them.

Finally I would like to mention Jenny Wilson, who had the Herculean task of refining my copy, and once again Emma Way, my editor, who gave me a free rein – or almost. Thank you.

Bibliography

Barker, Chris, *Mysterious Wales* (David & Charles, 1982)

Barker, Chris *More Mysterious Wales* (Paladin, 1987)

Barnatt, John, *Prehistoric Cornwall* (Turnstone Press, 1982)

Beckensall, Stan, *Prehistoric Rock Motifs of Northumberland* (Stan Beckensall, Hexham, 1991)

Beckensall, Stan, *Rock Carvings of Northern Britain* (Shire Publications, 1986)

Bergramar, Kate, *Discovering Hill Figures* (Shire Publications, 1968)

Bord, Colin and Janet, *A Guide to Ancient Sites in Britain* (Latimer, 1978)

Bord, Colin and Janet, *Ancient Mysteries of Britain* (Grafton, 1986)

Bord, Colin and Janet, *Earth Rites* (Granta, 1982)

Bord, Colin and Janet, *Mysterious Britain, ancient secrets of the United Kingdom and Ireland* (Paladin, 1972)

Bord, Colin and Janet, *Sacred Waters* (Granta, 1985)

Bord, Colin and Janet, *The Secret Country – More Mysterious Britain* (Paladin, 1986)

Burton, Antony, *The Shell Book of Curious Britain* (David & Charles)

Burl, Aubrey, *Prehistoric Stone Circles* (Shire Publications, 1979)

Chippendale, Christopher, *Stonehenge Complete* (Thames & Hudson, 1983)

Clarke, David, *Ghosts and Legends of the Peak District* (Jarrold, Norwich, 1991)

Cooke, Ian, *Antiquities of West Cornwall* (Men-an-Tol Studio, 1990)

Cooke, Ian, *Journey to the Stones* (Men-an-Tol Studio, 1987)

Crossing, William, *Stones of Dartmoor* (Quay, 1987)

Doren Stern, Philip van, *Prehistoric Europe from Stone Age Man to the Early Greeks* (George Allen & Unwin, 1969)

Dyer, James, *Discovering Regional Archaeology: The Cotswolds and Upper Thames* (Shire Publications, 1970)

Feacham, Richard, *A Guide to Prehistoric Scotland* (B. T. Batsford)

Green, Miranda J., *Dictionary of Celtic Myths and Legends* (Thames & Hudson, 1992)

Hadingham, Evan, *Ancient Carvings of Britain* (Garnstone)

Harlech, Lord, *The Illustrated Regional Guide to Ancient Monuments* (HMSS)

Hawkes, Jacquetta, *A Guide to Prehistoric and Roman Monuments in England and Wales* (Chatto & Windus, 1951)

Hawkes, Jacquetta and Lewinski, Jorge, *The Shell Guide to British Archaeology* (Michael Joseph, 1986)

Hawkins, Gerald, *Beyond Stonehenge* (Hutchinson)

Hayward, John, *Dartmoor* (Curlew, 1981)

Headley, Gwyn and Meulen, Wim, *Follies – A National Trust Guide*

Hebbert, Antonia (ed.), *Secret Britain* (AA, 1986)

Hutchinson, Geoff, *The Life and Times of John Fuller of Brightling* (1988)

Jones, Barbara, *Follies and Grottoes* (Constable)

Jones, Sally, *Legends of Cornwall* (Bossiney Books, 1980)

Jordan, Katherine, *The Folklore of Ancient Wiltshire* (Wiltshire County Council, 1990)

Kemp, Brian, *Church Monuments* (Shire Publications, 1985)

Knightly, Charles, *The Customs and Ceremonies of Britain* (Thames & Hudson, 1986)

Maciness, Lesley, *Anglesey* (Welsh Historical Monuments, 1989)

Mackie, Euan W., *Scotland Archaeological Guide* (Faber, 1975)

Marples, Morris, *White Horses and Other Hill Figures* (Alan Sutton Publishing, 1949)

Michell, John, *Megalithomania* (Thames & Hudson, 1982)

Miller, Hamish and Broadhurst, Paul, *The Sun and the Serpent* (Pendragon Press, 1989)

Muir, Richard, *Travellers History of Britain and Ireland* (Bloomsbury, 1983)

Page, Michael and Ingpen, Robert, *Encyclopedia of Things that Never Were* (Dragons World, 1985)

Pegg, John, *The Face of Dartmoor* (John Pegg Publishing, 1985)

Readers Digest, *Folklore Myths and Legends of Britain* (Readers Digest, 1973)

Richie, Anna, *Picts* (H.M.S.O. Edinburgh for Historic Scotland, 1989)

Richie, Anna and Breeze, David J., *Invaders of Scotland* (H.M.S.O. Edinbugh, 1991)

Richie, Anna and Graham, *The Ancient Monuments of the Orkneys* (Historic Scotland, 1978)

Richie, Graham and Harman, Mary, *Exploring Scotland's Heritage* (H.M.S.O Edinburgh, 1986)

Robinson, David M. (ed.), *A Mirror of Medieval Images* (Welsh Historic Monuments, 1988)

Sharkey, John, *Celtic Mysteries* (Thames & Hudson, 1981)

Tait, Charles, *The Orkney Guide Book* (Tait Photographic, 1975)

Thomas, Nicholas, *Guide to Prehistoric England* (Batsford, 1981)

Thomas, Tasmin, *Mysteries in the Cornish Landscape* (Bossiney Books, 1991)

Time Life Books, *The Celts: the Emergence of Man*

Time Life Books, *Feats and Wisdom of the Ancients* (1990)

Wainright, Richard, *A Guide to Prehistoric Remains in Britain* (Alison Hodge)

Walker, Charles, *Strange Britain* (Brian Trodd, 1989)

Walker, Peter N. *Folk Tales from the North York Moors* (Robert Hale, 1990)

Wheatley, Dennis, *The Devil and All His Work* (Hutchinsons, 1971)

Williams, Michael, *Curiosities of Cornwall* (Bossiney Books, 1983)

Williams, Michael, *The Moors of Cornwall* (Bossiney Books, 1986)

Wood, Eric S., *Archaeology in Britain* (Collins)

ST LEVAN'S STONE, *St Levan, Cornwall*

Little is known about St Levan, thought to have been a sixth- or seventh-century Celt. The famous stone lies in St Levan's churchyard, and it is said that it was his favourite seat after exhausting fishing trips. After one such trip, according to legend, he took his rod and struck the stone, which broke in two. He prayed over the stone and made a prophecy:

'When with panneirs astride,
A Pack Horse can ride,
Through St Levans Stone,
The World will be done.'

Time Chart

NEOLITHIC PERIOD 4500 B.C. to 2000 B.C.
Henge Monuments; Long Barrows

2500 B.C.	Beaker People
2466? B.C.	Noah's Ark, Book of Genesis
2200–1100 B.C.	Pyramid-building, Egypt
2000 B.C.	Wessex Culture

BRONZE AGE 2000 B.C. to 750 B.C.
Stone Circles; Holed Stones; Round Barrows; Stone Rows; Menhirs

1766–1122 B.C.	Shang Dynasty, China – 100,000 tortoiseshells and bones have been found, carved with the history and customs of the time
1102 B.C.	Homer of Smyrna – the *Iliad* and *Odyssey*
1000 B.C.	Sabaean kingdom, Arabian Peninsula – home of Queen of Sheba
776 B.C.	The first Olympiad
753 B.C.	Rome founded

IRON AGE 750 B.C. to A.D. 43
Hill Forts; Celtic Hill Figures; Pictish Culture; Druidism

552 B.C.	Temple of Diana, Ephesus
442 B.C.	Parthenon of Athens
296–263 B.C.	The Great Wall of China
A.D. 33	Death of Christ

ROMAN PERIOD A.D. 43 to A.D. 476
Roman Roads; Temples; Hadrian's Wall

First missionaries arrive in Britain to convert Celts

DARK AGES A.D. 476 to A.D. 1100
Dykes; Celtic Crosses; Holy Wells

A.D. 1000	Viking Chief, Leif Eriksson, discovers the east coast of America
A.D. 1066	Norman invasion of Britain
5th and 6th century	Saxon Britain
A.D. 570–632	Prophet Muhammad

MEDIEVAL PERIOD A.D. 1100 to A.D. 1500
Celtic Carvings in Churches; Cadaverous Tombs

A.D. 1492	Columbus reaches America

RECENT A.D. 1500 to Present Day
Neo-Druidism; Folly-building

Index